GASTRONOMY

by Jay Jacobs

Newsweek Books, New York

Frontispiece: Mosaic by Gaspar Homar

*Grateful acknowledgment is made for the use of excerpted material from the
following works:*
Between Meals by A.J. Liebling. Copyright © 1959, 1962 by A.J. Liebling. Re-
printed by permission of Simon & Schuster, Inc. and Russell and Volkening, Inc.
Food in History by Reay Tannahill. Copyright © 1973 by Reay Tannahill. Re-
printed by permission of Stein and Day Publishers, Associated Book Publishers,
Ltd., and Campbell, Thompson and McLaughlin Ltd.
Life and Leisure in Ancient Rome by J.P.V.D. Balsdon. Copyright © 1969 by
J.P.V.D. Balsdon. Used by permission of McGraw-Hill Book Company and the
Bodley Head.
The Rise of the West by William H. McNeill. Copyright © 1963 by William
H. McNeill. Reprinted by permission of the University of Chicago Press.

ISBN: Regular edition 0-88225-123-6 ISBN: Deluxe edition 0-88225-124-4
Library of Congress Catalog Card No. 75-2274
© 1975 Europa Verlag. All rights reserved.
Printed and bound by Mondadori, Verona, Italy.

Contents

1

The Essential Art

WITHOUT A SONG, a not altogether disinterested songsmith tells us, the day would never end. Perhaps not, but without breakfast it would hardly begin. Man can, and often does, live after a fashion without music, painting, sculpture, the dance, theater, literature—even love. Without food, he dies. Of all man's arts, gastronomy is the least dispensable, most elemental, most understandable, and most comforting. Not all the lullabies in the world will soothe the hungry infant, but the gaffer whose dancing days and amorous exploits are long behind him may still tuck zestfully into a hearty meal. As Jean-Anthelme Brillat-Savarin, the mayor—appropriately enough—of Belley and France's most celebrated gastronome, stated, "The pleasures of the table belong to all times and all ages, to every country and every day; they go hand in hand with all our other pleasures, outlast them, and remain to console us for their loss." Expressing the same sentiment a bit more succinctly, George Meredith wrote, "Kissing don't last; cookery do!"

To an extent unapproached by any other creature that has ever lived, man is omnivorous. Whatever it may be, from the ant to the whale (a far daintier feeder than himself), man will eat it if it doesn't eat him first. In his boundless voracity he will eat his food alive and squiggling, as shrimp are eaten in China's Hunan province, or after it has lain deep-frozen for aeons, as he has eaten hairy mammoth in modern times. He will eat whole species out of existence, as he has the passenger pigeon, and create new breeds in order to eat *them*. In his tireless quest for the edible he will prize open the most obdurate mollusk, pick the thorniest plant, root out the most esoteric fungus, savor the moldiest cheese, the most venomous reptile, the most malign tuber or improbable inner organ. At one time or another minorities among his number have been undaunted by the larvae of bugs, the spawn of eels, the fetuses of rodents, the eyes of sheep, the tongues of larks, the windpipes of pigs, the upchuck of whales, the brains of calves, the spittle of petrels, the guts of fish, and the gonads of asses, to mention a few items he has prized or still prizes as delicacies. There are those among him who devour roaches with relish, grubs with gusto, and pupae with

What ancient peoples ate—and why—tells us as much or more about their civilizations as the rest of their artifacts combined. The Minoan pot opposite, for instance, is decorated with fish and fowl, staple items in the diet of those seafaring islanders.

7

pleasure. Neither his dogs nor his cats have altogether escaped his appetite, and he has ingested his fellows with varying degrees of enthusiasm in various circumstances.

What he cannot put on his table man eats in fantasy, often applying to ordinary foods reverse euphemisms that transform veal rolls into "birds" or "headless larks" (*alouettes sans têtes*), licheelike fruits into "dragon's eyes" (*loong ngaan*), sausages into cold-blooded amphibians ("toad-in-the-hole"), and pasta into "straw and hay" (*paglia e fieno*). He also eats prairie oysters, Scotch woodcock, mock turtle, Welsh rabbit, "poor man's asparagus" (leeks, which on today's market often are dearer than the genuine article), and, around Venice, *polenta e oselèti scapài*, or corn meal with "little birds that got away." In imagination he will cannibalize his most respected women ("nun's thighs," "St. Agatha's breasts," and "nipples of the Virgin" are all eaten in Italy) and devour the "pope's nose." And in his subconscious hunger for second helpings he has devised a nomenclature of redundancy, giving his foods and culinary ingredients such names as couscous, *pili pili*, *shabu-shabu*, chowchow, *otak-otak*, boulaboula, baba, agar-agar, bonbon, tartar, *mahi mahi*, *'ndocca 'ndocca*, *titi*, *sari-sari*, *lolo*, and pawpaw.

With such culinary ingredients and thousands of others hardly more promising, he has constructed an art of infinite subtlety, exquisite refinement, and limitless variety. An art that has radically altered his appearance and the appearance of the world in which he lives, that has shaped his history as no other factor in that history has, and that demands the most direct and complete commitment of all his arts—gastronomy is the only art that engages all man's senses and most of his energies. It is an art to which he is indissolubly wedded from his racial genesis to extinction and throughout his individual journey from cradle to grave; an art built on appalling brutality and ineffable tenderness, of gut satisfactions and pure exaltation. An art of earth, air, fire, and water, of the very fabric of existence.

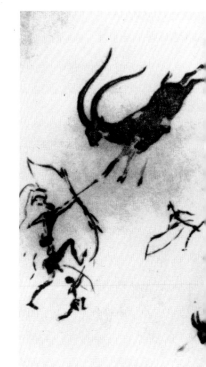

It was hunger that brought man's ancestors down from the trees and transformed them into what Desmond Morris felicitously has termed the naked ape. At ground level, preman gradually evolved from a largely herbivorous gatherer to a more sophisticated forager, developing a taste for insects and their larvae and small, slow-moving reptiles and mammals, supplementing his diet with whatever berries, roots, or the like that came to hand. At this stage of the game he was still a relatively dim-witted quadruped and might have so remained had his newfound appetite for meat not impelled him to stalk bigger, faster game after aeons of subsistence on easy prey. Intercepting a porcupine as it waddled along the forest floor was probably more painful than difficult. But making a meal of a quick, powerful feline carnivore—one that might have had similar designs on him—required a good deal more ingenuity on the part of our hero. The problem was how to kill at a safe distance. The solution, some three million years in coming, was to stand erect and let fly with a barrage of rocks.

As he learned to stand on his hind legs our still-simian forebear underwent a number of concomitant changes, salient among which were the increasing dexterity of forefeet that gradually evolved into

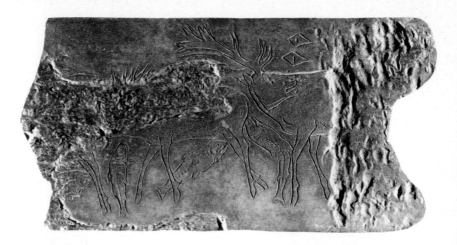

As recently as 9000 B.C., the preservation of food and the cultivation of crops were unknown—facts that reduced life to a ceaseless quest for fresh meat. To enhance his prowess as a hunter, Neolithic man frequently decorated both his cave homes and his weapons with images of his intended prey. Thus the wall painting at left depicts a wounded goat, and the bone fragment at right reveals etched outlines of deer and salmon.

tool-making hands and the imperceptible conversion of his teeth from weapons to food processors—a conversion that, coupled with the later recession of his jaws as he learned to soften his food by cooking it, ultimately was to transform him into a conversationalist of sorts.

"Tell me what you eat," Brillat-Savarin wrote, "and I will tell you what you are." Most of what little we know of earliest man is known from the remains of his meals. From bones found in his caves it is obvious that the hominid Peking man was a gregarious sort, probably capable of an intelligible grunt or two and certainly able to formulate a concerted plan of action, since he hardly could have brought down and lugged home such prey as buffalo and rhinoceroses singlehandedly.

We know he used fire some 360 millennia ago, for light and warmth, but probably remained ignorant of its culinary possibilities. (The discovery of quantities of charred bone in his caves has led some theorists to conclude that Peking man roasted his meat. The conclusion is dubious at best, since only incredibly inexpert butchering or thoroughly carbonized meat would produce much charred bone. Moreover, there is clear evidence that he split marrow bones to get at their content—a laborious operation that cooking his meat would have obviated and that in any case yields a far less tasty product. In all likelihood the scorched bones found among Peking man's effects had been used, once they were stripped of raw meat, to fuel his fires.) We know, too, that his diet included wild mutton, pork, and smaller game but consisted mainly of venison, and that on occasion he also ate the flesh of his fellows. Finally, we know that his conversion to a largely carnivorous diet freed early man from the burden of having to eat his way through his waking hours, enabling him to cultivate other interests. Meat, with its high protein concentration, takes about a third the time to provide the same nourishment as herbivorous matter.

Other primitives tended fires at other times (cave dwellers in southern France perhaps as early as 750,000 years ago), but no clear evidence establishes when men began deliberately to cook their food. Whenever it may have been, it was doubtless the result of accident, as a scrap of meat left too close to, or clumsily dropped into, the fire was found to be tastier, easier to chew and to digest, and more comforting than a hunk of cold, bloody venison, otter, or whatever. For aeons thereafter, though, plain roasted meat remained the highest—indeed the only—form of cookery; and no culinary advances were to be made until the

At the end of the Neolithic epoch, man's search for sustenance was to benefit from three vital discoveries. The first of these was the domestication of animals; the second, the cultivation of plants; the third, the invention of pottery. The last of these was in many ways the most important, for it enabled man to preserve and store food, brew and transport beverages, and bake bread. The graceful pottery bird at left, created in Asia Minor in the eighth century B.C., held fluids in its hollow body. The more utilitarian vessels at lower right are Cretan.

Paleolithic era, when the people of the Aurignac region of southern France seem to have hit on the notion of wrapping their food in wet leaves and steaming it over embers, a technique that later was to be independently discovered in other parts of the prehistoric world. Until Neolithic man began to make pottery vessels some 7,000 to 12,000 years ago, as the last of the glacial incursions receded, this was about as far as cooking had, or could have, come, a rudimentary stone griddle and the occasional use of pit-cooking notwithstanding.

It was in the Neolithic epoch that man's methods of feeding himself underwent the first and most fundamental of the innovations that were to culminate in the advent of civilized life on earth. With the retreat of the glaciers and moderation of the climate, three profound changes, all directly concerned with man's desire to eat well and regularly, occurred: the discovery that certain animals could be domesticated, the deliberate cultivation of edible plants, and the development of pottery.

Of these three changes, the first made man independent of the uncertain migratory patterns of wild beasts, assuring him of a more regular meat supply, eventually adding milk and its derivatives to his larder, and laying the groundwork for his later revolutionary use of draft animals and beasts of burden. The second enabled him to develop the settled communities prerequisite to any kind of advanced civilization. The third enormously enlarged the scope of his culinary efforts, making it possible for him not only to add considerable variety to the ways in which he prepared his foods, but to add significantly to the number and types of foods in his diet (and, consequently, to his survival potential), to develop the arts of fermentation and preservation and, in time, to bake his daily bread. In combination these factors resulted in a population explosion that transformed mankind from an insecure and insignificant minority to a dominant species that would one day exercise control over all species on earth.

In view of man's agonizingly slow progress from his earliest appearance until Neolithic times his subsequent achievements, and the havoc he has wrought, the works of a relative twinkling, are truly astonishing. Despite our new awareness of and putative concern for the ecology, ecological problems are anything but new. And while many of us tend to see them as the products of such very recent phenomena as heavy industrialization and quantum population growth, the fact is that man hardly had learned to walk before his efforts to feed himself had begun drastically to change almost every aspect of the world in which he lived. By scratching the earth with a pointed stick he set in motion processes of topographical, biological, and climatic alteration beside which the effects of all his wars together (thus far at least) are as nothing. Of all the actions of all earth's creatures, none has had anything like the effects of man's striving for a full belly. To that end he has leveled vast forests, decimated seemingly inexhaustible herds, laid barren incalculable tracts of fertile soil, and upset oceanic balances. To that end he has traveled improbable distances, adapted himself to almost intolerable environments, waged murderous wars on his own kind, invented his gods, and put his very continuance in jeopardy.

There is little scientific agreement as to how, when, and where the Neolithic revolution took place. In all probability, however, several peoples of the New Stone Age learned the rudiments of farming and stock raising independently, at different times, and in such scattered portions of the world as the Near East, Central America, and what is now Thailand. In her book *Food in History*, Reay Tannahill advances the theory that settled communities, at least in the Near East, did not lead to agriculture but were the result of agriculture. This came about when men discovered the uses of wild grain, which must be harvested quickly once it ripens; this required their presence nearby "not only in readiness for the moment of harvest but also because, after it, a return to distant caves would hardly be practicable for a family encumbered— in days before either draft animals or the discovery of the wheel—with a commissariat weighing over 2,000 pounds."

The earliest manufactured food doubtless was grain paste, a crude prototype of the *pulmentum* (itself not very sophisticated) whose use the Romans were to learn from the Etruscans, and which remains a staple (*polenta*) in much of Italy today and is still eaten in one form or another in many other parts of the world. As ingested in Neolithic times, grain paste made from grasses that would eventually evolve into wheat, barley, and millet took a not-altogether-appetizing form that might be approximated today by moistening cracked wheat with water. Early threshing was an arduous and uncertain procedure, and it is safe to assume that a good deal of indigestible chaff and bran was consumed along with the nourishing grain itself.

Even today, chemically untreated "natural" grains contain minute eggs that will hatch larvae if kept unrefrigerated for any length of time. If Neolithic man's sensibilities were bothered by the presence of these intruders in his porridge he didn't trouble to record his misgivings. In all likelihood he welcomed them as savory additions to a monotonous diet. With or without an admixture of animal life, grain had one great advantage: it could be stored for future use, thereby freeing its user from constant concern about where his next meal was coming from and leaving him time for the manufacture of tools and artifacts. (It also freed his mate from abject dependence on his hunting skills; it was she, no doubt, who harvested much of the grain, toasted it on heated surfaces to split open the husks, and ground it into groats. And if her male was kept indoors by the weather or returned empty-handed from the hunt, he was in no position to berate her with cries of "What? Grain paste *again* tonight?")

If the portable nature of grain increased man's mobility—an advantage chiefly to nomadic herdsmen—it also decreased his need to travel long distances in search of game. As a consequence Neolithic man became for the most part a settled creature. It could not have taken him many seasons to realize that it was from seeds like those he threshed and ate that future crops sprang, that by overharvesting one year's growth he diminished the next, and that by strewing these magical seeds wherever he chose he could, within certain limitations, raise his food wherever he chose. Gradually but inexorably Neolithic man became the master of his own destiny; no longer a gatherer but a cultivator, a breeder of his own stock, an artisan—and an artist.

As man spent more time in the immediate vicinity of his hearth, he began to learn its many uses. He discovered in the north of Europe that smoke was a natural preservative of fish, and there or elsewhere he learned that it enhanced the keeping properties of meats. Various cultures found that grain, roots, and vegetables could be made digestible —and palatable—by cooking them in heated water, although this was a cumbersome undertaking before the invention of pottery vessels, requiring stone-lined pits or such inefficient containers as hollowed rocks, large shells, or the stomach bags of ruminants.

At his hearth Neolithic man—or, more likely, woman—also discovered that grain paste took on an appetizing crustiness if left awhile on a hot stone and that clay turned to a stonelike substance when exposed to fire. With these two discoveries—bread and pottery—man's process of

Mankind's first manufactured food was a grain paste made by threshing and grinding primitive grasses. With the discovery that this paste could be rendered more edible by slow baking on a hot stone, bread came into existence. Man was no longer merely feeding, he was eating—and in settled communities in great river valleys, the first gastronomical revolution occurred. Man the hunter was supplanted by woman the baker (left), and haphazard food gathering by the systematic storage of foodstuffs (top) and beverages (above).

civilizing himself began in earnest. Both added immeasurably to the variety of his menu, allowing him to combine ingredients in entirely new ways, while pottery vessels made possible an efficient means of boiling and added simmering, stewing, braising, oven baking, and perhaps a rudimentary form of frying to his culinary repertory. He was no longer a mere feeder, but an eater. Moreover, he had begun to learn how to eat and, by Brillat-Savarin's definition, was on his way to becoming an intellectual.

Man had tamed the wolves that later were to become his dogs while still primarily a hunter. The domestication of goats and sheep (probably in that order) began in the Near East around 10,000 B.C., probably when these untrammeled ruminants threatened his grain supply by browsing the fields in the spring, when the tender new shoots of wild cereal grass appeared. The pig and aurochs (the ancestral cow) were subdued around 7000 and 6000 B.C. respectively, when men found they could keep them in or near their own settlements, where the aurochs proved useful not only as a source of fresh meat but, like the goat, as a provider of milk and a powerful adjunct to the labor force. Sheep, though, were another matter, requiring vast tracts of grazing land and creating a new class of nomadic herdsmen—men who moved out of the settled areas in search of greener pastures and who, in turn, created new communities in previously unsettled regions. In the older settlements, a more or less predictable annual food supply inevitably led to increases in population that just as inevitably produced waves of emigrants who further extended man's domain, taking their seed and livestock with them and introducing new forms of life into regions that sometimes were and sometimes were not prepared to support them.

In some of the invaded areas imported grains drove native strains out of existence. In cooler climates where their wheat would not grow, men were forced to adapt their diets and cuisines to such wild grasses as rye and oats. (That such changes may have been traumatic in many cases can be surmised from the unhappiness with, and resistance to, the exotic foodstuffs with which undernourished populations are being provided by more fortunate nations today.) Around the older settlements intensive agriculture led to runaway proliferation of insect and animal pests, the stripping away of extensive tracts of forest, and the ultimate exhaustion of the soil. Even before the end of the prehistoric epoch, man's insatiable hunger had in many parts of the Near East replaced fertile green lands with windblown, shifting sands. Elsewhere, as in the Nile valley, the reverse was true.

But wherever man penetrated, he perforce ate. The consequences of his appetite were sometimes malign, sometimes benign, but always, always, the world in which he lived was different for his having fed himself on its bounty. To put a construction on the lines that Andrew Marvell certainly didn't anticipate, his ". . . vegetable love should grow/Vaster than empires, and more slow." So would his love of meats and fish, of fowl and spices. And with it, empires would wax and wane, the face of the earth would be subjected to unending change. In it, the destiny of all life under the sun would ultimately be caught up.

2

Feasts for the Gods

Pray, now, my guest, to the lord Poseidon, even as it is his feast whereon ye have chanced in coming hither.

The Odyssey

FROM EARLIEST TIMES, man's first duty has been to his gods. For the most part, those gods have been made in man's image, and, by a curious coincidence, the form of propitiation they have most often demanded has provided man with one of his least onerous tasks. Indeed, the celebration of the ritual feast is his sole universal pleasure and most accessible art form. In all probability, it is also the oldest. As the nineteenth-century historian Fustel de Coulanges noted, "To eat food prepared upon an altar was, to all appearance, the first form which men gave to the religious act."

In many Western cultures, the religious and ceremonial connotations of feasting have been largely forgotten, but ancient forms linger on, shaping the ways in which men eat on any level above that of mere subsistence. However unwittingly they may do so, the Englishman disjointing his Sunday roast, the Parisian gourmand exulting in the tenderness and delicate savor of his *primeurs*, the coveted first vegetables of spring, and Dagwood Bumstead raiding the refrigerator to concoct some monstrous sandwich in the dead of night, all are playing out scenarios whose ritual origins go back to the dawn of human life on earth.

As primitive man had worshiped fertility figures, harvest goddesses, fire gods, and the like, so many of civilized man's early deities were intimately involved with the production, preparation, and consumption of food. The goddess Ninkasi, for example, was to the Sumerians she "who fills the mouth." In India, as in Greece and Rome, the god of the hearth, the nourisher and provider, was the most familiar and most demanding of the deities. In Egypt, Osiris, who reigned over human death and rebirth, naturally doubled as the god of grain, dwelling in the realm of the dead between the fall harvest and spring planting. Prometheus not only enabled the Greeks to cook their meat by bringing fire from the sun (wrapped in a fennel stalk, thereby anticipating the salient characteristic of the modern French culinary classic, *loup de mer flambé au fenouil*), but encouraged them to reserve choice portions for themselves, leaving the gods to weary their jaws on tougher cuts.

Once they had availed themselves of the Promethean sanction (con-

The ancient Egyptians, whose elaborate funerary rites are without historical parallel, made immensely thorough preparations for dining in the hereafter. To ensure that the deceased did not lack for succor on his dark journey, he was provided with symbolic provender in the form of highly detailed tomb paintings depicting feasting scenes.

veniently devised by themselves), it was an easy step for the Greeks to reverse altogether the ancient ritual of the sacrifice. This had begun with the ceremonial slaughter of a beast and its symbolic consumption by a god, which is to say, by fire. If the god in question happened to be a bit off his feed on a particular day and failed to consume the whole beast, well, what harm if mere mortals helped themselves to some left-over roast mutton? And since the Greeks had great respect but not much love for their gods, once they'd acquired a taste for godly viands it would have been a simple matter to dampen the appetites of their deities by stoking the sacrificial fire with a little less wood. And then progressively less, until one day the sacrificial sheep, ox, or whatever, instead of being scorched to the bone, came through its ordeal fit only for human consumption—that is, done to a turn.

In such a manner or close variants thereof, the ritual feast originated in Greece and elsewhere. In Egypt, for instance, sacrificial bulls were stuffed with bread, honey, fruits, and aromatic resins, then burned with great ceremony. Whatever remained when the fires died down was eaten by the celebrants. Since they had taken the precaution of fasting for some time before the event, it's safe to assume that the gods' share was quite small. (While most forms of ritual feasting originated in some such fashion, a few may have derived from more macabre rites. The pages of the *Iliad*, *Odyssey*, and other ancient sagas are as pungent with the aroma of roasting meat as an American suburb on a midsummer weekend. Much of the feasting described takes place immediately after victories in battle, and it would not be unreasonable to speculate that rites of this sort may have been atavistic vestiges of the cannibalistic victory orgies of some prehistoric epoch; revels sanctified no doubt by invoking the name of some deity.)

The step from ritual feast to gastronomy was a logical progression. For gastronomy, quite simply, is the art of good eating and, in any meaningful sense of the term, originated during the classical Greek period. People ate well before then, to be sure. Existing evidence indicates that a meal much like the New England clambake (one of the American Indian's innumerable contributions to gastronomy) may have been known in the Ukraine at least as long ago as 25,000 B.C., and it might well be argued that the first human to stuff a fistful of sweet, sun-warmed berries into his maw was at that moment eating as well as anyone has since. The Assyrian king Merodach-baladan raised both domestic fowl and aromatic herbs in the eighth century B.C., presumably in full awareness of their culinary compatibility. The early Baby-

The ritual of the sacrifice originated as a means of propitiating the gods, but it quickly became an excuse for public feasting. In pharaonic Egypt, for instance, sacrificial bulls (lower left) were stuffed wth bread and honey, then slow-roasted on pyres. This practice presumably satisfied the tutelary gods of the Nile valley—and it unquestionably satisfied the hungry faithful. The basic diet of the Egyptian peasant—beer, bread, and onions —rarely varied, but the upper classes enjoyed a wide range of edibles (above). The top register of the tomb painting opposite shows fowlers working the lowland marshes alongside the Nile; below, grapes are pressed, ducks dressed, and fish caught for the tables of the wealthy.

lonian kings held truffles in as high esteem as Brillat-Savarin did in the nineteenth century, and Babylonian supremacy in Mesopotamia is supposed to have come to its end even while Belshazzar feasted "before the thousand" on honeyed barley cakes and other delicacies.

Egyptian rulers, though less profligate at table than their counterparts elsewhere in the ancient world, washed down their mullet caviar, roast goose, and roast veal with potent beer (having first eaten boiled cabbage as a preemptive measure against drunkenness), sopped up the remnants of their hearty stews with any of some thirty distinct varieties of flat and leavened breads, and concluded their repasts with fresh dates and rich pastries. Banquets of a hundred courses marked the birthdays of the kings of Persia, and King Solomon on one occasion followed the ritual sacrifice of sheep and oxen with a modest little dinner party that didn't break up until fourteen days after the guests—all male—had assembled.

The occasional high quality of individual dishes and the quantitative magnitude of the individual feast notwithstanding, eating in the ancient world remained for the most part a hit-or-miss affair, and it wasn't until the late sixth century B.C. that the first conscious efforts were made to transform simple gluttony and catch-as-catch-can feasting into the art that later came to be known as gastronomy. The metamorphosis began in Athens, when professional cooks were called upon to systematize and orchestrate the banquet and where the first sauces worthy of the name were developed.

Most scholars agree that in hymning the praises of red meat and making it the staple diet of his heroes, Homer was on solid historical ground. The warriors whose exploits he chronicled half a millennium after the fact were not too distantly descended from nomadic tribes-

Having dined in life on such delicacies as caviar and quail, pigeon stew and beef ribs, the elite of Egypt were determined to feast as well in the afterlife. To this end their tombs were embellished with bas-reliefs like the one seen above, in which a moveable feast of livestock and fowl is borne into a crypt by teams of servants. The cultivation of grain is a necessary first step in the brewing of beer, and it is not illogical that the first of the true grain harvesters, the Sumerians, should also have produced nineteen varieties of highly potable "bread beer." On the tomb relief at right, an Assyrian servant pours a special libation for his king.

18

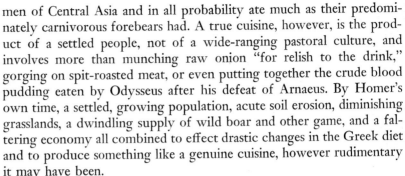

men of Central Asia and in all probability ate much as their predominately carnivorous forebears had. A true cuisine, however, is the product of a settled people, not of a wide-ranging pastoral culture, and involves more than munching raw onion "for relish to the drink," gorging on spit-roasted meat, or even putting together the crude blood pudding eaten by Odysseus after his defeat of Arnaeus. By Homer's own time, a settled, growing population, acute soil erosion, diminishing grasslands, a dwindling supply of wild boar and other game, and a faltering economy all combined to effect drastic changes in the Greek diet and to produce something like a genuine cuisine, however rudimentary it may have been.

That it was a rudimentary cuisine is well documented. Homer may not himself have eaten the robust fare he described with such undisguised relish, but his mouth obviously watered at the thought of the plain red meat ingested by his heroes when they weren't forced to make do with messes of pottage. Clearly, a hunk of roast meat, a bit of unleavened bread, and a communal kylix of watered wine represent the most exalted gustatory experience he was capable of envisioning, and later writers of the classical period weren't precisely enchanted with his idea of good eating. Admittedly there is something ludicrous about the notion of an Achilles or a Diomedes sacrificing a sardine or a domestic hen to a Poseidon or a Zeus, but both fish and fowl are conspicuously absent from the poet's works, although both doubtless graced his table far more often than meat.

Indeed, by Homer's time the use of meat was largely restricted to the tables of the rich and the communal ritual banquet. In the heroic era, the banquet had been a somewhat democratic affair attended by all social classes, although women participated only as servants and the cuts of meat offered swineherds and beggars were, as might be expected, slightly inferior to those served to the political, religious, and social upper-crust. The meal was preceded by prayers and incantations, the rinsing of the guests' hands by girl slaves, and the service of an apéritif of Prammian wine (not unlike Tokay or muscatel) mixed with grated goat cheese and dusted with barley meal, a singularly unappealing concoction by today's standards, perhaps, but one the Greeks of the period—no great drinkers anyway—appear to have enjoyed. This was followed by what today would be called a dip of onions, honey, and barley paste and then the meat, which invariably was spit-roasted over wood embers, accompanied by flat bread, and washed down with heavily watered wine (the usual ratio was one part wine to three of water, a formula devised in Homeric times and continued down to the last days of the Roman Empire).

It would be an exaggeration to say that the communal feasts of the gods represented the only chances the Greek peasant of the late archaic and early classical periods got at a square meal. In general, however, he wasn't eating very high off the hog, the infrequent slaughter of a domestic swine notwithstanding. With the exception of feast days, he saw little meat and subsisted for the most part on grain or bean pastes, gruel, and, less frequently, goat cheese and a few figs. Although olives constituted his chief crop, they were often his sole cash crop and, with wine, Greece's major export commodity. Therefore they and their oil were used sparingly at the point of origin. Overcultivation of the olive, incidentally, combined with overtimbering to devastate the Greek landscape, decimate the cattle, sheep, and big-game population, all but wipe out the production of grain, and ruinously affect the peasant economy. Ultimately, it deprived Greece of its self-sufficiency, making it dependent for its subsistence on the importation of foreign foodstuffs—a factor that has had much to do with the Oriental character of even the present-day Greek cuisine.

If the peasant's diet was monotonous, the contemporaneous rich city dweller's was hardly less so. The rich man's diet was regulated more by choice than necessity however; and if his meals tended toward sameness, it was because he had better things to do with his time—or so he imagined—than fritter it away on the pleasures of the table. His daytime sustenance took the form of quick snacks, usually alfresco, while the evening meal was nothing much more than a bothersome prelude to a night of good talk, with tongues loosened by wine. Simple as his meals may have been, though, they were epicurean alongside the standard fare of the Spartan, whose salty pork broth thickened with barley and laced with vinegar was a standing joke throughout the ancient world, its ingestion deemed a fate worse than death.

With the emergence of Athens as the preeminent city of classical antiquity, Greek culinary affairs took a marked turn for the better, at least insofar as the well-to-do were concerned. The classical Athenian prided himself on his refinement and, just as the Corinthian superseded the simpler Doric and Ionic orders of the archaic period, all aspects of his life—and particularly gastronomy—were characterized by greater elaboration, more fanciful forms, more rarified connoisseurship. Athenaeus, a sedulous chronicler of the social, gastronomic, and intellectual life of the later classical period, records no fewer than seventy-two varieties of bread then in use, curls a lip at the barbaric stew of the Spartans, takes the old heroes to task for their ignorance of such elementary niceties as vine-leaf garnishes, and fills fifteen books with the record of a single dinner party. Eubulus earlier had contrasted Attic fastidiousness with the indiscriminate gluttony of the Boetians (who, with their still-extensive pasturage, were the only remaining Greeks able to raise and enjoy beef in quantity), and all Athenians looked down their noses at the tosspot Scythians. Feasts were still held for the gods, but now the gods had better watch their table manners.

Social dining had taken precedence over ritual feasting in the life of the cultivated Athenian and, just as the worldly modern American may gorge ritualistically on plain, traditional fare at Thanksgiving, Christmas, and Easter but dine on frenchified delicacies the rest of the year, so the Athenians dutifully wolfed red meat on holy days but on other occasions regaled their friends with peacocks' eggs, Copaic eels in beet leaves, land snails, cockles, mussels, and other dainty morsels—so much so that one old-school trencherman, Lynceus, castigated them for serving only a succession of appetizers that in no way managed to "satisfy the belly."

Moreover, fundamental changes had taken place in the very forms

It was the ancient Greeks, with their twin passions for elegance and order, who both elevated and systematized the art of eating. In sixth-century B.C. Athens, the ritual sacrifice (above) was but a prelude to the banquet—at which quantities of spit-roasted beef were consumed. To wash down such repasts the Greeks drank watered wine—the beverage being offered Dionysus, the god of drink, on the urn at near right. Wine and olive oil were the major export commodities of ancient Greece. Carefully packaged and weighed (far right), these coveted liquids were then shipped to all parts of the Mediterranean Sea.

traditionally associated with eating. Whereas the Homeric heroes and Greeks of the archaic period had planted themselves four-square in chairs to partake of meat butchered and roasted by themselves or their priests and served at communal tables, the Athenians, perfumed and festooned with garlands, reclined on couches to nibble at exotica prepared, with all manner of canting assurances, by Sicilians or other imported professionals. To be sure, a few morsels were cast on the hearth to give the gods a taste of the good life before the meal commenced, but these were a far cry from the thick "thigh slices" burned on folded fat of which Homer tells us.

"Who loves thee," counseled Hesiod, "summon him to thy board." The leisured Athenian often spent a good part of his morning at the Agora, extending or wangling dinner invitations. For the man of decent means, giving a symposium meant renting extra furniture on the day in question and hiring entertainers. A professional cook was also engaged for the day, usually an officious Sicilian who declared himself the master of a science involving all manner of arcana and of whose tyranny the kitchen slaves were to be thoroughly sick by evening's end.

Diners reclined two to a couch, ate from small portable tables and, strictly speaking, partook of either two or three courses, although each course might consist of myriad little dishes designed to show off the full range of the cook's virtuosity. When there were three courses, the first might have consisted of such hors d'oeuvres as fish roe, oysters, anchovies, onions (roasted in ashes and sauced with a mixture of honey, goat cheese, herbs, sesame oil, and vinegar), sea urchins, cockles,

smoked sturgeon, a "sweet wine sop" (Lynceus), radishes in oil, boiled cabbage, fresh cucumbers, asparagus, peas (often pureed and served over eggs), turnips, beans, and garlic. The last was served as a vegetable in its own right; coupled with a prodigious intake of raw and cooked onions, it must have prompted many an Athenian wife to give thanks to the gods for her exclusion from the festivities.

Red meat, as has been noted, wasn't much in evidence, but pork seems to have been something of a main-course showpiece at any really big blowout. A domestic pig that had eaten itself to death was considered a rare treat and one document refers to a culinary *tour de force* in which a whole pig was roasted from one end to its middle, boiled the rest of the way, and stuffed with such imaginative delicacies as bird entrails and sow's womb. Chicken, duck, and fatted goose also varied the menu, as did small game, particularly hare. (Archestratus, the Brillat-Savarin of his day and the first of a long line of pedant-gastronomers, abandoned his wonted preciosity to proclaim the superiority of roast hare, served hot from the spit and seasoned only with salt, over the thickly sauced preparations then in favor.)

Fish, however, was much preferred to both flesh and fowl, although here, too, Archestratus tried hard to dim the enthusiasm of his compatriots by putting all sorts of strictures on its use. Salt Black Sea tuna, for example, although popular and accessible, was beneath contempt, and any self-respecting host would not only serve fresh tuna imported from Byzantium, but abjure any not caught at the time "the Pleiad is setting." Ray, Archestratus insisted, must be served boiled at midwinter with a dressing of cheese and asafetida (a noisome relative of the carrot now used medicinally as an antispasmodic but inexplicably favored as a condiment in ancient times); harp fish had to be either boiled or roasted, depending on the color and texture of its flesh; dogfish (sand

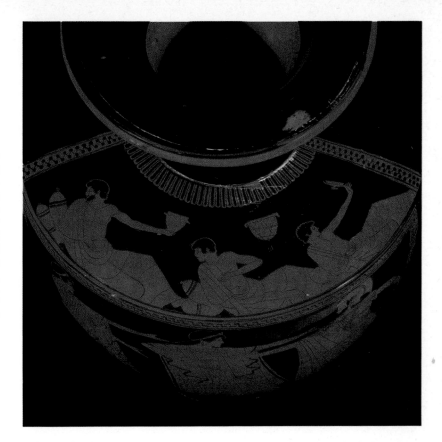

By 500 B.C., virtually every eastern Mediterranean civilization was producing its own vin ordinaire, *but none could compare with the superior vintages bottled on the Greek islands of Chios and Lesbos. These sweet wines, fermented in resin-soaked vats, were favored for private feasts as well as public rituals. At right, an example of the former; at lower left, an instance of the latter: Helen fills a kylix for Priam, king of Troy.*

shark) could be seasoned with cumin and little else if roasted, but boiled with fragrant green herbs—and so on, and on.

Sole, roast lamprey, conger, mackerel, red mullet, turbot, halibut, carp, sardines, fried anchovies, sturgeon, roast young shark, squid, octopus, swordfish, crab, and crayfish, all served in adhesive sauces of one sort or another, might also figure as entrées, along with blood sausages and, less frequently, a roast kid reeking of asafetida. Food was eaten with the fingers (making the use of thin, runny sauces impractical) and bread was used as a sop, pusher, and napkin. A common cup, or kylix, of wine was passed from guest to guest.

Although any modern oenophile might have trouble swallowing them, Greek wines—especially those from Chios and Lesbos—were for centuries the finest the ancient world had to offer and, after the olive, Greece's major export. Uncut, they were often thick as molasses and nearly as potent as today's hard liquor, and only the infamous Scythians downed them neat. Since fermentation wasn't then the precisely controlled process it later came to be, the raw grape juice was mixed with a variety of preservatives ranging from condensed sea water to liquid resin—a substance that imparts a distinct bouquet of turpentine to the *retsina* still drunk in Greece. Then, as now, connoisseurs extolled the virtues of old wines, although the practice of leaving them to mature in smoky lofts must have imbued them with the robust aroma of frying bacon. In general, the reds were the strongest and sweetest and the whites more insipid, although a pale golden variety was favored by those who enjoyed a relatively dry wine.

After a break during which the guests' hands were again rinsed,

fresh garlands were distributed, and more wine was poured, the banquet's last course was served. This consisted of fresh and dried fruits, nuts, sweetmeats, and a variety of spiced honey cakes accompanied by ceremonial sips of undiluted wine from a common goblet and toasts to "the good genius." That out of the way, the real business of the evening, the symposium (often but not always a euphemism for a sustained drinking bout) got under way.

Popular legend notwithstanding, the orgiastic feast, complete with fire-eaters, acrobats, naked dancing girls, and erotic tableaux, was a late improvement on Athenian dining etiquette that was introduced by Alexander and his Macedonians. For the most part, the banquet in classical Athens was a decorous affair (after all, it was held within earshot of the host's wife and family), usually with a flute girl or two performing discreetly in the background. But while the food served was distinguished by a variety and a degree of attention to the finer points of gastronomy that previously had been unknown, Greek dining of the classical period fell far short of real distinction.

It remained for the Romans to develop the full-blown orgy and a truly sophisticated cuisine, although they, too, have been given more credit by posterity than they probably deserve. "Upon what meat doth this our Caesar feed," asked Shakespeare's Cassius, "that he is grown so great?" As it happened, the noblest Roman of them all was happiest when eating plain field rations with his troops.

Other Romans were not as simple in their tastes. The precocious boy-emperor Elagabalus, for one, who before his murder in a privy never spent less than 100,000 sesterces on dinner, literally smothered guests under avalanches of flowers, entertained the survivors with gladiatorial combat, and whored in his bath between courses of ostrich brains and peacocks' tongues. Gaius Caligula, for another, one of whose gastronomic soirées produced a tab of ten million sesterces. Apicius, the father of the cookbook, reduced to ten million sesterces after eating his way through ten times that amount, decided he couldn't possibly dine in style on that and took his life. The emperor Claudius regularly invited as many as six hundred freeloaders to a night of guzzling and gorging, and one of his successors, the gluttonous Vitellius, was particularly partial to a modest dish of his own devising, "The Shield of Minerva"—an improbable mélange of flamingoes' tongues, peacocks' and pheasants' brains, the sex glands of lampreys, and pike livers—and is

reputed to have sent fleets in search of its components. Then there was Lucullus, whose very name implies gastronomic ostentation.

"Men eat to vomit," complained Seneca, "and vomit to eat." Their dishes, he went on to note, were fetched from the farthest corners of the known world and then not even digested. Caesar's tribune Sallust described his contemporaries as "slaves of their stomachs" and Ammianus Marcellinus likened the men of Rome to "a flock of starving and screeching peacocks" who waited on tenterhooks for their food to cool. In an era of cheap slaves and expensive horses, a good slave-cook (once the lowest of the low) might cost three times the price of a mount but only a third of what was paid for a choice fish. Still, all things are relative, and the Roman, perhaps not without envy, deplored the big-bellied Etruscan, whom he called "*obesus*," for his "unbridled luxury and indolence" and indiscriminate postprandial lovemaking.

Of course, not every citizen of imperial Rome lived in the grand manner. For every voluptuary there were countless starvelings who eked out a marginal existence with the help of the *annona*, a form of public assistance whereby free grain was distributed to the poor, and whose diet, like that of their Greek counterparts, consisted almost in its entirety of grain pastes and water. But for most Romans of any means whatever, gourmandism was a way of life; so much so that various sumptuary laws were enacted—if not very zealously enforced—in sporadic attempts to save the populace from its own appetites. As the British historian J.P.V.D. Balsdon has noted:

26

Although Rome's less affluent citizens were obliged to subsist on an unvarying diet of coarse rye bread and watered wine, the city's markets did offer a tempting array of fresh produce to the monied. Quinces, harvested locally (near left), were but one of the dozens of varieties of fresh fruit sold from trestle tables (far left) in the city's markets. Domestic and imported wines (below) were widely available, and butcher shops sold beef, pork, and game (top right), as well as poultry and eggs (lower right).

The normal Roman's fondness for food is a historical fact which has to be faced. Fortunes were squandered on food by men "who lived for their palate alone," men whom Seneca regarded as the most deplorable of all spendthrifts. In extreme cases grossly expensive eating led in the end to bankruptcy; men unable even to afford the price of a rope to hang themselves with signed on as gladiators and, with no option, ate gladiators' rations. Apart from spectacular victims of sensational greed, men of all kinds . . . were fascinated by gourmandism.

As Balsdon also notes, not all dinner parties were orgies, or all dinners parties. At a typical formal dinner of relatively modest scope, nine participants occupied three couches arranged in a U-shape around a central table: these were the *summus lectus*, the *lectus medius*, reserved for the more distinguished guests, and the *imus lectus*, occupied by the host and members of his family. In bold outline, the service plan conformed to that of the Greek three-course banquet—with appetizers offered as a *gustatio*, or first course; followed by the *mensae primae*, or main course (often divided into the *cena prima, secunda,* and *tertia*); and dessert *(mensae secundae)*. Guests were bathed with scented soaps on arrival and, from about the time of Tiberius onward, drinks were offered before dinner—often to guests who had managed to get themselves well-sozzled in the course of a leisurely afternoon at the baths. *Mulsum*, a wine-and-honey apéritif, was served with the *gustatio*, which would be made up of raw and cooked vegetables, various kinds of salt

27

fish and shellfish, olives, land snails (fattened to the point where they were too big for their shells), oysters from East Anglia or from the Lucrine Lake, where they were scientifically cultivated, urchins, sliced eggs, mixed green salads, and the like.

For the *mensae primae* the cook was expected to pull out all the stops. Although a good many Roman cookbooks survive, it's difficult to tell just how the dishes of the main course tasted. For one thing, most recipes have little to say about weights and measures. For another, some essential ingredients are no longer in use (asafetida and pyrethrum, for example, aren't likely to turn up on the shelves or in the freezer of your local specialty shop, let alone the supermarket) or even in existence; the herb silphium, *de rigueur* in most dishes, became extinct around the middle of the first century. Then too, while the Roman gourmet may have scoured the earth for exotic viands, many of them must have been quite rank by the time they reached his table—a condition that affected their savor to an indeterminable degree and may account for the Roman predilection for smelly sauces.

Whatever their flavor may have been, the usual components of the main course included the best fish available, various kinds of small game from the Laurentine forests, peacocks, plump capons and other domestic fowl, roast boar ("born for the table") stuffed with thrushes, and a *pièce de résistance*: a whole pig from Gaul, seasoned with pepper and cumin and slit open with great ceremony at the table to reveal an abundance of assorted sausages. *Pâté de foie gras* soaked in milk and honey was a much-favored delicacy, as were pigeons fattened on premasticated bread, and force-fed dormice glazed with honey and rolled in poppy seeds. Tuscan cheeses would be served, along with the udders of virgin sows, pork testicles, Spanish pickles, and, on particularly auspicious occasions, ostriches or camels from the African provinces. Indeed,

Fish, both fresh and salted, was a staple of the Roman diet. Above: a fishmonger cleans Black Sea tuna, a delicacy much prized by Rome's elite. Opposite: a Pompeiian mosaic displays the fruits of the sea, avidly consumed by the empire's epicures.

even elephant didn't escape the notice of some epicures, who found only the trunk to their liking, while at the other extreme the tender flesh of suckling puppies in the elder Pliny's day was considered food fit for the gods.

Most dishes were elaborately sauced, often with *liquamen*, an odoriferous concoction so much in demand that it was factory-made in various towns throughout the empire. Made of salt fish and old wine, it developed its full cheesy character after deliquescing for two or three months in the hot sun, must have stank to high heaven at full throttle, and was indiscriminately used with fish, meat, and game. A sauce recommended by Apicius as an accompaniment to cold chicken contained *liquamen*, olive oil, vinegar, mustard, a decoction of fresh grape juice, and dates, along with dill, mint, and the ubiquitous asafetida. Oriental spices—pepper in particular—were used as liberally as a household

could afford, and one is left wondering how the principal ingredient of any dish could be distinguished under such an onslaught of relishes and seasonings. (A recent theory suggests that many affluent Romans suffered from lead poisoning, an affliction that renders the palate insensitive to any but the strongest flavors.)

The wines available to the Romans were far superior to any known to the earlier Greeks. Although women banqueters were expected to drink only *passum*, a sweet raisin wine on which they often managed to get thoroughly squiffy despite its putative low potency, male diners availed themselves of such highly esteemed products of the vintner's art as the Falernian, Alban, Nomentanum, and Sorrentine wines of Italy, along with others from the Rhône and Rhine valleys, Syria, and Spain. The best of the Greek wines from Chios and Lesbos also were popular despite—or perhaps because of—their great cost. Bread, of course, was eaten with the *mensae primae*, but was not used to clean the fingers, as it was in Greece, since linen napkins were in common use.

The dessert course was essentially what it had been in Greece, except that such exotic fruits as Libyan pomegranates, Armenian apricots, Syrian pears, Persian peaches, and the like supplemented the limited home-grown options of the Greeks, while confections were likely to be far more sophisticated and designed more fancifully. Priapic constructions were a source of never-ending amusement and set pieces in general were devised with an ingenuity probably unsurpassed until the eighteenth century, when the vaunted French chef Carême was to boast that his decorative pastries were the highest form of architecture.

At their feasts, the Romans still paid lip service to the conventional gods. It is obvious, though, that what they worshiped above all else was their bellies. With the decline of the empire, however, moderation became the watchword and it was to be a long, lean time before the religion of excess underwent a revival.

The Roman mosaic detail above, although fanciful in spirit, is essentially accurate in its depiction of the process of harvesting and pressing grapes. Only the vines themselves are freely rendered— as a tangle of lacy tendrils whose riches are plucked by naked cherubim. At right, a subtly colored still life from the wall of a Roman residence.

eus in adiutorium meum inten
de.
Domine ad adiuuandum me
festina.

3

With Renewed Zest

These seigneurs, when they want to eat, take the meat up with a silver fork.

Jaques le Saige (1518)

I observed a custome in all those Italian Cities and Townes . . . [that] is not used in any other country that I saw in my travels . . . the Italian[s] . . . doe alwaies at their meales use a little fork when they cut their meat.

Thomas Coryate (1611)

ALTHOUGH THE FRENCH MASTER CHEF CARÊME would one day diagnose it as "essentially barbaric," classical Roman cooking had been characterized by pretensions to sophistication and an enthusism for experimentation that might soon have allowed it to evolve into a grand cuisine. But with the breakup of the empire and with the barbarian sweep across Europe in the fifth century, gastronomy in Rome itself and—such as it was—in the Roman provinces suffered a severe setback. With trade severely curtailed, the various regional cuisines could no longer be enriched with foodstuffs and seasonings from outlying sources, and diets again became insular and monotonous. Large-scale desertion of cities and towns inevitably resulted in a simpler, less indulgent and less informed life-style. Even worse off than usual, the peasantry subsisted on whatever it could scratch from the earth, forage from nearby woodlands and streams, and preserve or store for use during the long, barren winters. Feudal communities enjoyed only what they could produce within the safety of their own confines. In and around Rome, the classical Roman style persisted, but the use of spices and other exotic condiments was drastically curtailed. Eating in Europe in the following centuries went through some very dark days, with classical traditions all but obliterated and with crude feast and rampant famine marking the parameters of what might be termed a gastronomic holding action.

Throughout history the lives of the rich, the powerful, and the literate have been well documented, but the vast majority of the world's inhabitants have been born, suffered, and died in obscurity. As a consequence, the diet of the medieval poor is largely a matter of conjecture. Langland's Piers Plowman tells us he can afford neither pullets nor geese, pork nor eggs, but finds consolation nonetheless in his two green

For centuries after the fall of Rome, the art of eating well— like virtually every other art— was to make negligible advances. First barbarian hordes, then the Black Death were to disrupt the normal pattern of life in Europe. Even among the wealthy (opposite), banquets were austere: courses were few, ingredients unvaried, and spices minimal.

33

cheeses, a few curds, cream, an oaten cake, two loaves of bean and bran,
parsley, leeks, "many cabbages / And besides a cow and a half." Piers,
of course, lived in the fourteenth century, a time of relative stability
and prosperity, the Black Death notwithstanding. His forebears may
not have had it so good.

In the ninth and tenth centuries, for example, an already marginal
rural existence was in no way bettered by the depredations of maraud-
ing Vikings, who scourged everything in their path except livestock—
which they expropriated for their own use. During the same period,
rye, the staple crop in much of northern Europe, often was infected
with a fungus that left thousands suffering from St. Anthony's fire, or
ergotism, an affliction that in its more benign manifestation led to mass
insanity and, in its more acute form, to the decimation of communities
that innocently had partaken of their daily bread. To the south, a form

FLUUIUS ape ILENA

gesLaua RALIS

SCS MARTINUS

Repeated barbarian invasions of Europe eventually drove uncounted thousands of city dwellers back to the land, where subsistence was less precarious. The Carolingian manuscript at left, devoted to the labors of the months, depicts such mundane tasks as tilling the soil, harvesting wheat, and slaughtering hogs. During the Dark Ages the great monasteries served as citadels of civilization in every sense. These completely self-supporting communities brewed their own liquors, raised their own livestock, and grew their own herbs. Many also included a vivarium *(above), a tank in which fresh fish could be kept until they were needed for the table.*

of wheat rust (rust parasites were unwittingly carried in barberry bushes introduced by invading Arabs) resulted in widespread crop failure and famine. Famine, whatever its localized cause, was a specter that haunted medieval Europe.

When the peasant wasn't literally starving, the mainstay of his diet, in northern Europe at least, was coarse rye bread. When wheat was available (which wasn't often), it was husked and steeped in warm water to produce a glutinous porridge called frumenty. This might be eaten cold with milk and honey, or warmed up with scraps from the family cauldron, a catchall utensil kept continually on the simmer, its contents replenished from day to day with whatever came to hand—a rabbit smuggled home under a cloak, a bit of salt pork, a small bunch of root vegetables, a few turnip greens, a cabbage, and the like. In short, this was a monotonous diet of soft, overcooked foods, varied perhaps with seasonal or dried fruits, an occasional fish (usually poached in more ways than one), wild spring greens, and pease porridge. For a few days in November, when most stock was slaughtered for want of winter fodder, stringy fresh pork, served throughout Europe at Martinmas, provided an auspicious start to a winter that might culminate in acute hunger as nothing grew and supplies ran out.

The poor saw little or no beef. "Why should the villeins eat beef, or any dainty food?" a noble poet asked rhetorically, concluding that "Nettles, reeds, briars, peashells are good enough for them." The peas-

35

ant might keep one or two cows for their milk, however, usually on condition that the landlord received their calves in payment for their pasturage. In any case, cattle were valued chiefly as draft animals. Pigs were thin and stunted by modern standards and their meat was tough, but they could be raised with little care or expense. Those beasts that survived the annual Martinmas slaughter spent the winter nights in the cottages, where their body heat dispelled some of the chill and their mingled odors became an unnoticed but comforting element in a life with precious few comforts.

The cauldron, or stockpot, which was emptied and scoured only at the beginning of Lent, was peculiar to the north, where timber still abounded and long-burning fires were both necessary and feasible. Ultimately, it was to provide the basis for French cooking as we know it today. In Italy and along the Mediterranean, where widespread metal smelting had depleted the forests, the small charcoal fire with its relatively low heat necessitated the development of different utensils and different culinary techniques. The ubiquitous veal *scallopine* of the modern Italian repertory, for example, sliced as thinly as possible, further flattened, lightly sautéed, and sauced with a simple modification of its pan fat and juices, owes its existence to the exigencies of early medieval cooking in the south as surely as the classic French *pot-au-feu*, *tripes à la mode de Caen*, or countless slow-simmered soups and sauce bases trace their origins to the cauldron of the north. Indeed, the two most distinctive modern European cuisines, the French and the Italian, spring respectively from the pot and the skillet; from medieval concerns with slow and quick cooking.

The life of the poor didn't improve appreciably as the chaos of the early Middle Ages slowly was supplanted by a semblance of order. In the monasteries and the great halls of the nobles, however, beef and other "dainty" foods were eaten in quantity, although the adjective seems somewhat inappropriate in the light of contemporaneous descriptions. Charlemagne, by all accounts the nearest thing to an epicure his period produced, invited women to his table (with the gallant proviso that "they did not offend with nauseating odors nor noxious perfumes")—a custom that was soon to fall into desuetude, there to remain until its revival by Catherine de Médicis in sixteenth-century France.

Although his courtiers favored mulled wine, a putative aphrodisiac, as an apéritif, Charlemagne—the father of some fifty children by various wives and mistresses—preferred Norman cider, which he believed prevented gout. His meals began with mixed green salads and consisted chiefly of copious helpings of spit-roasted meats, game, and fish, accompanied by fruit compotes and eaten with the point of a knife. The *pièce de résistance* of his coronation banquet and other great occasions was a roast peacock in full panoply, served with flames issuing from its beak, and by all accounts as flavorless as it was tough.

Some descriptions would have it that Charlemagne, a physical giant even by modern American standards, ate as he drank: in moderation. If so, the mind boggles at the relative appetites of his small-statured contemporaries. Even though breakfasts in general were a lot heartier in the eighth century than they are today, the man who casually

It is hardly surprising that the dedication of the monastery of Royaumont (above) included a multicourse banquet, for few thirteenth-century Europeans ate as well as those living in cloistered orders. The peasant population existed on a monotonous diet of coarse rye bread and mushy porridge, both made from stone-ground grains (right).

destroyed a full wheel of cheese and a joint of venison first thing in the morning can't be said to have been toying with his food. Nor can the man who responded to his doctor's advice to take it easy by calling for three roast geese and a rump of boar.

His gustatory capacities—and a reputation for serving nut-stuffed dormice at banquets—notwithstanding, two more "serious" claims are usually advanced on behalf of Charlemagne's pretensions as the first gastronome of northern Europe: his recognition of the excellence of Brie cheese and his practice of using bread to catch the drippings of his heaped-up roast game. More to the point, he was responsible for a widespread program of agricultural reform, extensive reclamation of barren lands, and the promotion of viniculture. Less directly but perhaps more importantly, he fostered the proliferation of the abbeys, and it was within their cloistered precincts that tenuous contact with the traditions of classic Rome was maintained, where a systematic approach to the production and storage of food was worked out, and where the highest forms of medieval cookery were developed.

As the Vikings stepped up their depredations, the abbeys, islands of tranquil productivity, welcomed the traveler with the best meals then available anywhere in Europe and fed the peasant, somewhat less lavishly, in times of need—a form of relief for which he paid dearly at other times, when monk, landlord, bishop, and ruler alike extracted regular tribute from him.

A well-operated abbey, such as that of St. Gall in Switzerland or St. Nicolas-lès-Cîteaux in France, was a city unto itself and eminently self-sufficient. It boasted its own kitchens and herb gardens, orchards, mill, bakeries, breweries, wineries, distilleries, butteries, cellars, smokehouses, coopers' shops, and storehouses, along with "stews," or vivaria (a Roman invention), stocked with live fish, and coops, sheds, and pens for a variety of domestic fowl and animals. Its inhabitants, of course, observed frequent fasts and meatless days, although such meat as that of poultry, beavers, frogs, and unborn rabbits (one of the more imaginative specialties of classical Roman gastronomy) were conveniently classified as fish. Nonetheless, the image of the plump, rosy-cheeked medieval cleric, so popular with later genre painters, had many a real-life counterpart. As one saturnine observer noted; "Flocks and fleeces, crops and granaries, leeks and potherbs, drinks and goblets are nowadays the reading and study of monks."

As had been the case in classical antiquity, religiosity in medieval Europe as often as not was a convenient cloak for gourmandism. Whether the primary objective of the Crusaders was to liberate the Holy Land, enrich themselves on the fabled treasures of the East, or indulge in a good peripatetic feed is debatable. But their horses, according to Peter of Blois, were "laden not with steel but with wine, not with spears but with cheeses, not with swords but with wineskins, not with javelins but with spits." One would think, he added, "they were on their way to a feast, and not to a fight."

Medieval castles and manors, no less than monasteries, were islands of self-sufficiency, although game was more often the meat of kings and nobles who, lacking the cleric's access to the literature of the past

T aut itrencha de hyaumes taut ipcha defaus   T li dus le feru fans vifee t fans outrage.

(and in many cases simple literacy), soon reverted to a sort of gastronomic barbarism after a brief flirtation with Roman niceties. To understand fully the nature of the secular banquet in the medieval north, three factors must be borne in mind: the participants were not sedentary types, but physically active men who spent their days riding, hunting, hawking, and often fighting; the drafts and dankness of the halls they came home to after strenuous days outdoors could be dispelled only by huge roaring fires; the evening meal (usually begun in the late afternoon) often was taken as close to the source of warmth as possible and constituted the day's great diversion, a multimedia happening whose degree of variety, ingenuity, and ostentation also served as a measure of the host's wealth and puissance. The banqueters, then, were cold, hungry athletes, filling their bellies for both nourishment and warmth with robust, stick-to-the-ribs fare and delighting in the theatricality of dishes that in some cases were "sotelties" (subtleties) not meant to be eaten and, in others, ornate *tours de force* that bordered on the inedible. Moreover, a roaring fire would have made culinary finesse an impossibility even had the diners harbored a taste for delicate sautés or fine sauces. The sweating turnspit worked as close to the fire as was physically possible. For the cook, the measured adjustments and gentle stirring of a sophisticated cuisine were literally out of reach.

Any number of fastidious modern writers tell us of tables blanketed in flowers and succeed in conveying an idea of medieval banqueting as an extension of the gentle, stylized cult of courtly love. In actuality, it was anything but that. From all surviving evidence, a typical big feed must have borne a startling resemblance to a football game played on a muddy field, with the pungent effluvia of ill-disguised rancidity lending a certain piquancy to the proceedings. Until the wooden trencher came into widespread use late in the Middle Ages, a slice (*tranche*) of stale bread was shared by each couple for use as a plate. This doubtless took on a spongelike porosity as soppy foods from the cauldron successively were heaped onto it, leaving a spreading puddle of mingled fats and drippings at each place.

Forks, of course, were unknown, as were napkins, and neither knives nor spoons were always adequate to the job at hand. To judge from surviving rules of etiquette, the most efficient tools, the fingers, were washed ostentatiously before the meal began. They might, however, then travel regularly from serving bowl (where they could disappear up to the elbow in pursuit of an elusive morsel) to platter to *tranche* to mouth; from mouth to some intimate part of one's or one's

In northern Europe, where firewood was plentiful, virtually all foods were cooked in the same giant caldron (above), a capacious cast-iron vat that rarely left the spit and suffered cleaning only at Lent, when for forty days no meat was eaten. Well into the fourteenth century, customers brought their own dough to the local baker (below), who shaped it into loaves and slid it into his brick ovens on long wooden paddles. The setback that European cuisine suffered during the millennium after the fall of Rome is belied by the elegant alfresco banquet depicted in the fifteenth-century manuscript illumination opposite.

partner's anatomy—gentlemen were exhorted not to claw openly at their "codware"—and back again, digressing along the way to explore a nostril or an ear, search out a head louse, be licked "clean" by a scavenging dog, or retrieve a fallen portion from the rush-strewn floor.

Jugglers, acrobats, and troubadours took over in the intervals ("entremets") between scrimmages, and a particularly impressive dish —say, an oily swan in full gilded plumage with a camphor-impregnated wad blazing in its bill—would be presented with a blare of trumpets. Conversation was loud and in all likelihood ribald, and less decorous sound effects may have been much in evidence. Old sources are vague on the subject of belching, which may or may not have been considered good form (as it still is among the Arabs), but united in their condemnation of both manifest and surreptitious flatulence from the "hinder part"; a condemnation so often voiced that one suspects the writers had plenty to rail against. As the modern food historian Reay Tannahill observes, suppression may not have been easy: the three main vegetables of the Middle Ages were beans, cabbage, and onions.

As trade with the East—spurred by the Crusaders' fascination with the spices they found there—gradually opened up, monotony and rancidity were mitigated to some extent, at least at the tables of the rich. Still, quantity remained the salient feature of the medieval feast and menus remained disorganized, utterly lacking in orchestration, and numbingly repetitious. In 1393, for example—shortly after the appearance of northern Europe's first manuscript cookbook and two years before its author, Guillaume Tirel, was buried beneath a shield emblazoned with three cookpots—a Parisian banquet was comprised of twenty-one dishes exclusive of sweets. It included three eel preparations, three roasts, five kinds of simply prepared fish, two beef marrow dishes (both served as parts of a single course), two kinds of fritter, and two dishes made with cut-up chicken. An English menu drawn up six years later for the marriage feast of Henry IV lists thirty-eight dishes aside from subtleties. Of these, no fewer than six were aquatic or wading birds (cygnets, herons, cranes, bitterns, egrets, curlews), all similarly prepared and hardly distinguishable from one another. Five were simply roasted game birds, and five were domestic fowl. In other words, there were sixteen kinds of bird, with only one, presented in a mousse of chicken, prepared with any imagination. Such was the state of gastronomy north and west of the Alps before Catherine de Mèdicis's arrival in France.

On the other side of the Alps, the situation was far more promising. Despite the barbarian invasion of the fifth century, the Romans had maintained political control over a substantial part of Europe and, even as this gradually melted away, their cultural heritage—and, by extension, the Greek heritage—lingered on in Italy. And if Carême was later rightly to characterize Roman cooking as heavy and unrefined, the Romans had made a start of sorts, converting what had been Greek cookery into a cuisine of relative sophistication.

As Waverley Root remarks in *The Food of Italy*, modern Italian cooking was built on foundations provided by the Greeks, the Etruscans, and, to a somewhat lesser extent, the Saracens. "Each of the three," he writes, "left behind a specific trademark. That of the Etruscans was a sort of mush made from grain which at times had the consistency of porridge and at others that of a crumbly cake. It does not sound like particularly inspiring food, but on it the Romans conquered the world." To the Greeks Root assigns the fish chowder that came to be called *brodetto* along the coasts of Italy (and *bouillabaisse* in Marseilles); to the Saracens the flaky, multileaved pastry that appeared in Europe in the eighth century and eventually took the form of *baclava* in the Near East, *pastilla* in North Africa, *pastel* in Spain, *Strudel* in Central Europe, *mille-feuille* in France, and in Sicily and Naples *millefoglie* and *sfogliatelle* respectively. Later, the Saracens were to make other, less voluntary contributions, as the Crusaders returned with spinach (a vegetable that, like most vegetables, is still exploited more successfully in Italian cookery than any other), rice (a good Italian *risotto* has no equal, French and Oriental claims to the contrary notwithstanding), cane sugar, sweet oranges, lemons, sherbet, marzipan, and buckwheat, to mention a few.

Other cultures, of course, contributed to medieval Italian cooking —the Romans had imported pork sausage from Gaul and the Normans brought the salt cod Italians call *baccalà*—but the effects of their contributions were, and remain, generically minimal. More important, perhaps, to the evolution of Italian cookery were the peasant's tendency— natural enough in the warm south—to munch a few raw onions, turnips, olives, or a bit of garlic *al fresco* and the previously mentioned need for quick-cooked dishes. To this day, Italians prefer vegetables crisp and undercooked and pasta *al dente*, or resistant to the bite.

Although *bistecca alla fiorentina* is one of the world's vaunted steak preparations, from Roman times onward the Italians have not been great beef eaters. Their historical preference has been for veal and pork, both pale meats and both from smaller animals whose flesh, in an age without refrigeration, could be consumed with relative dispatch, while much of it was still fresh. Moreover, most of the Italian boot lies within comparatively easy range of the sea and fresh fish. As a consequence of these factors, once the classical Roman predilection for exotic foodstuffs (and the long journeys their importation required) became an altogether impractical matter, foods in Italy have tended to be far fresher than elsewhere in Europe.

The Italian peninsula suffered a chronic fuel shortage from the beginning of the Christian era, when its forests were logged over to provide fuel for ironmongers' forges. To compensate for this deficiency the Italians were to develop a highly specialized cuisine that involved minimal cooking. The hogs being slaughtered at top left, for instance, were destined for the skillet, not the stewpot. At left center, a winetasting session; at lower left, nobles dine on crayfish, another entrée requiring little cooking. The preparation of tripe (right), on the other hand, necessitated hours of stewing —and quantities of fuel such as only northern forests provided.

The art of eating well was to enjoy its own renaissance in fifteenth-century Italy. In the environs of Florence, for example, a renewed enthusiasm for the pleasures of the table was to produce scenes such as the one at left in which dairy cattle are being milked and cheese produced. These dairy products subsequently would find their way to the picnic tables of nobles throughout Tuscany (below).

Fresher food, in turn, meant that even when Eastern spices again began to become accessible, they lacked the tremendous appeal in Italy that they enjoyed beyond the Alps, where their primary functions were to disguise rancidity and lend variety to the monotonous fare of the cauldron and the spit. Coupled with the fuel shortage already discussed, all this combined to produce a far simpler cuisine than most, and one that concentrated on the inherent nature of its ingredients. Whereas spices and sauces both were agents of obfuscation in northern European cooking, in Italy spices were used much more sparingly than the preferred herbs and only to accentuate, not cloak, the nature of the principal ingredients. The primary role of sauces was to moisten dry

dishes and lend interest to such bland, neutral substances as pasta and *polenta*. From earliest times, Italian cooking has tended toward regional diversity, often with little resemblance between the cuisine of one town and its insular neighbor, let alone between the north and south. But if Italian cooking can be said to have unifying characteristics, those characteristics, at least since the dissolution of the Roman Empire, have inclined increasingly toward freshness, integrity, simplicity, lightness, and a reliance on recipes that convert raw materials into finished dishes with a directness that has its closest counterpart in the cooking of China and Japan.

The origins of pasta are obscure. Popular legend would have it that Marco Polo brought the first noodles back from China. Some theories credit the early Etruscans and others with its independent invention, and it's easy enough to visualize its fortuitous discovery by more than one housewife who, after flattening a strip of dough for one purpose or another, trimmed it with a knife, accidentally dropped a curl of the trimming into a simmering pot, retrieved it after it had cooked awhile, and found it to be edible. Later, dried pasta could have been discovered in much the same fashion, when some homemaker was distracted from the preparation of fresh pasta for the evening meal (let's say five-year-old Gonzago chased a neighbor's pig into the woods, got himself utterly lost, and became the object of a prolonged search), returned to

44

her kitchen to find that her handiwork had dehydrated and, either by accident or experimentation (perhaps based on previous experience with dried cod), found that cooking it produced much the same results as those achieved with the moist product.

In any case, pasta hardly could have failed to appeal to those Italians whose eating habits were formed by the Etruscan *polenta* tradition. *Maccheroni* (that is, flat noodles, not the factory-produced tubular macaroni of modern times) was firmly established as a staple food in various parts of Italy by the later Middle Ages, and documents on spaghetti, including official papal dicta concerning its quality, survive from the thirteenth century. Of course, the tomato sauce that later was to become ubiquitous in the south was to remain unknown, not only during the Middle Ages but throughout the Renaissance. Other sauces were known, though. A simple sauce of oil and garlic—still one of the tastiest ways of dressing pasta—had been around since antiquity; the affinity for pasta of some version of the various pounded herb sauces called *pesto* must have been recognized early in the game; a white clam sauce very like a number of modern preparations must quickly have found favor as an accompaniment to noodles along the coasts; and a prototype of the modern classic *fettucine Alfredo* is described in *The*

Forme of Cury, an English cookbook of the fourteenth century. Indeed, there is very little that doesn't go well with one type of pasta or other—a happy circumstance the late medieval Italian was quick to recognize.

The fork—an implement without which many types of pasta hardly could be eaten—had been introduced to the Venetian court in the late eleventh century by the Byzantine wife of the doge Selvo. At the time, it didn't take Venice altogether by storm, possibly because the lady in question insisted on being fed from it by a eunuch slave. It reappeared in the same city in the fourteenth century, however, at a time when the table manners of the Italians had attained a degree of fastidiousness unheard of in the rest of Europe. Its use soon spread throughout the peninsula, if nowhere else. (England, an adamant holdout, was to remain unenlightened until the sixteenth century, when the tool enjoyed a brief vogue at the court of Elizabeth I. It was then consigned to limbo for another century and regarded with suspicion for a couple more.)

As the Middle Ages ran their course elsewhere in Europe, men and women continued to eat roasted meats from the points of their knives or on spikes (it was customary for a guest to bring his own utensils) and to scoop wet foods from their trenchers with spoons, their fingers, or their cupped hands—techniques that made for a limited culinary repertory comprised of thickly sauced, custardy preparations called mortrews, the garnished gruels known as frumenties, thinner concoctions named brewets, soups (usually served with bread sops), and a dreary procession of markedly similar pasties, meat pies, and the like, which had the singular advantage of presenting meat and moisturizers in a tidy, manageable, self-contained package.

In England after 1066 French cooks were favored at court, but it should be remembered that French cooking was then a much more primitive business than it later became, and its chief contribution was linguistic, adding such terms as "veal," "mutton," "pork," and "beef" to the vocabulary. Whale meat—especially from the tail—was a delicacy that in the reign of Edward II was reserved, with sturgeon, for royalty. Royalty also favored lampreys, to the ultimate detriment of Henry I, who ate himself into his grave on a surfeit of their indigestible flesh. Richard II, an advanced gourmet for the fourteenth century and an unstinting host who is reputed to have served thousands of guests at a time, liked oysters poached in Greek wine, highly spiced gravies, and the curiously named mawmenee, a questionable mincemeat made up of pheasant, cinnamon, ginger, cloves, sugar, and wine.

The cuisine that Catherine de Mèdicis brought to France in 1533 when she became the bride of the future Henri II was the cuisine of Tuscany and, more particularly, Florence. Catherine, whose family had made much of its fortune in the spice trade, landed in France with an

When Catherine de Mèdicis traveled to France in 1533 to wed Henri II, she brought with her a unique dowry: the refined and imaginative cuisine of Tuscany. The superlative dishes and exquisite sauces of her homeland were to captivate the French, who enthusiastically adopted Italian dishes and dining style.

47

astonishing retinue of cooks, bakers, and confectioners, a battery of kitchen equipment such as never had been seen in that country, and an unbridled appetite for her native foods: elegantly sauced milk-fed veal, *piselli novelli* (which the proprietary French much later were to dub *petits pois*), crisp broccoli, juicy tournedos, "royal" carp, truffles, cocks' combs, kidneys, sweetbreads, *quenelles,* and such caloric innovations as artichoke-heart fritters, pasta, *zabaglione* (rechristened *sabayon* in France), "iced creames," rice pudding, frangipane tarts, macaroons, and a fruit- and nut-filled layer cake called *tarta balconata.*

A modest culinary tradition had been building up in France since the accession of the Valois kings in 1328, but Catherine's arrival on the scene signaled a gastronomic renaissance that eventually was to culminate in the most sophisticated cuisine the world has ever known. It also marked the introduction of the fork into the transalpine world—an event that was to change not just dining etiquette but the very nature of gustatory proclivities throughout Western Europe—and heralded a profound change in the character of the state banquet. This, as staged by her prospective father-in-law, François I, had been little more than a prolonged drinking bout shunned by the women of the court. Under Catherine, the French court was transformed into a "little Florence" and the banquet became a coeducational—and far less bibulous—affair at which her notorious Flying Squadron of high-born temptresses flagrantly displayed charms that must have grown increasingly convex as the ladies strove to follow the example of their epicurean queen.

Whatever else she may have been, Catherine was a daughter of the Renaissance, an epoch that changed the art of gastronomy no less than it changed all the other arts and, indeed, the very fabric and tenor of Western civilization. The cuisine of the Renaissance was restrained, disciplined, natural, and unpretentious; a cuisine that has been attributed by Waverley Root and others to "the sober Etruscan spirit"—an evaluation that might bestir the bones of classical Romans, who considered their own gastronomical excesses mild by Etruscan standards. As Root remarks of the emerging Renaissance Florentine:

> He wanted quality, and his character saved him from confusing quality with extravagance. When he emerged from the heaviness and gluttony of the Middle Ages, whose cooking was a prolongation of that of the Roman Empire, he did not return to that Empire as an exemplar of the classical world of which he was again becoming conscious, but to the austere Republic, with its simpler, healthier food.

To appreciate the distance the gastronomy of Florence and its environs had come by the onset of the Renaissance—and how little it resembled the gluttony of the north—a glimpse at the diet of the fourteenth-century Tuscan merchant Francesco Datini may be instructive.

As the Italian Renaissance spread northward, it sparked an exchange of commodities as well as ideas—and within a short time the markets of Europe (above left) were stocking spices and produce from the far corners of the Continent and beyond. The cuisine of the south remained superior for some time, however, and it is said that the Tuscan merchant Francesco Datini, the largest figure in the painting detail at right, ate better than most of Europe's · monarchs.

Although well able to afford almost limitless ostentation, Datini dined simply and well, his preferences running to delicate veal dishes (eaten on the advice of his doctor), which he enjoyed sautéed with a touch of garlic, garnished with a type of small mushroom (*Clitopilus prunulus*, locally called *prugnoli*) that throve around his native Prato, served with fresh young garden beans on the side, and preceded by either soup, *lasagne*, or *ravioli*, any of which he dusted with Parmesan cheese. In short, a balanced, nutritious meal such as is served today in millions of Italian homes and thousands of Italian restaurants.

Datini took two meals a day, one in the morning and another around dusk. This was the custom in and around Florence, as it had been in much of Europe from antiquity onward. (Not all of Europe, to be sure. In England, in particular, as many as four meals had come to be considered a normal day's intake by the time the Renaissance reached that scepter'd isle.) His meals differed little from those of the average middle-class Tuscan, who might begin dinner with a green salad, be served a small fowl, pasta, or a liver-filled crêpe as his entrée, and wind up the proceedings with fruit or cheese—again, a meal that seems natural enough by today's standards. Meat was reserved for special occasions (when it often took the form of roast kid, as it does in Italy today), as were such sweets as rice puddings and simple tarts. (The more complex forms of pastrymaking didn't develop until the early fifteenth century, shortly before Catherine de Mèdicis introduced them to the French.)

Such were the sensible eating habits of the early Renaissance; habits that weren't to change appreciably with time as far as the Florentines were concerned. A taste for luxury and exoticism arose in the early fifteenth century, was suppressed for a time, and reasserted itself after

The diffusion of Renaissance ideals had its impact upon all social classes, even the lowest. By the late fifteenth century, for instance, the peasant population of Western Europe was supplementing its bread and porridge diet with a variety of cheeses (left), white breads, and superior local wines (right).

Savonarola became the *pièce de résistance* of one of history's more celebrated cookouts. That it didn't really produce much in the way of overindulgence—at least by earlier Roman standards—is indicated by widespread clerical railing against those sybarites who were not content to eat their pasta plainly boiled as God had meant it to be eaten, but insisted on converting it to macaroni au gratin.

Moderation has never been a patch on excess as a literary and historical attention-getter. Consequently we hear little today of the restraint and sobriety that characterized Renaissance gastronomy in the main. Instead, we hear for the most part of Medici, Valois, and Tudor ostentation; of Henry VIII of England, stuffing himself like a Strasbourg goose, spitting in his finger bowl, blowing his nose into his napkin, and behaving in general like some grotesque Rabelaisian infant.

It is Henry, not Datini, whom the historical novelists and the filmmakers remember, for it isn't Datini's elegantly simple, enviably civilized dinners that make the stuff of legend. Rather, it is Henry's prodigious overindulgence in immoderately spiced and sweetened roasts— and a cholesterol intake that turned a natural athlete into something resembling the capons he so gleefully devoured. It is such spreads as

51

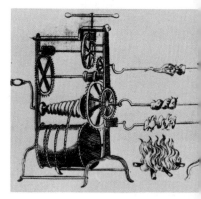

that which the city of Paris laid on for Elizabeth of Austria in 1571 that live on in history.

The day of the event being Friday, no meat could be eaten, but the assembled guests somehow got by on a couple of barrels of oysters, one thousand pairs of frogs' legs, four hundred herring, two hundred crayfish, fifty carp, twenty-eight salmon, eighteen brill, ten turbot, innumerable steamed mussels, and uncounted broiled lobsters. Oh yes, there was a fifty-pound slab of whale meat on hand lest anyone find the daintier provender inadequate.

And then there were the modest tuck-ins staged by Pope Pius V. As described by Bartolomeo Scappi, who wrote one of the earliest printed cookbooks to appear in Italy, one of these comprised just two courses from the credenza and two from the kitchen. The courses, in order of appearance, consisted of marzipan, Neapolitan spice cakes,

Instrumento per levar ogni gran caldaro dal focho

Not illogically, Renaissance Italy, which produced the first great European cuisine, also produced the first printed cookbook. Written by Bartolomeo Scappi, it emphasized cooking techniques as well as menus and recipes. The illustrations for Scappi's book include: the detailed interior of a typical Tuscan kitchen (far left); a multitiered roasting spit (near left); and an ingenious caldron hoist (right). Such refinements spelled the end of semibarbaric feasting of the sort depicted below.

more marzipan, Malaga wine with Pisan biscuits, puff pastries, prosciutto cooked in wine and served with capers, grapes, and sugar, wine-braised salt pork tongues, cold roast songbirds garnished with their own tongues, fresh grapes, Spanish olives; fried sweetbreads and calves' liver in an eggplant sauce, spit-roasted skylarks with lemon sauce, quail with eggplant, lemon partridge, sweetbreads and ham in puff pastry, sweet-and-sour poultry, roast stuffed pigeons, roast rabbit in sauce, thickly sliced spit-roasted veal *au jus*, legs of goat in *their* roasting juices, an almond-paste soup garnished with three pigeons per serving, meat jelly, boiled fattened geese with slivered almonds, cheese, sugar, and cinnamon, stuffed boiled breast of veal with a fresh-flower garnish, parsleyed new-born calf, almonds in garlic sauce, rice cooked in milk, sugared and dusted with cinnamon, stewed pigeons with *mortadella* sausage and whole onions, cabbage-and-sausage soup, chicken pies (with two chickens per pie), fricassee of kid with fried onions, large custard pies, boiled calves' feet with cheese and egg; bean tarts, tarts of candied pears, quince pastries, assorted fresh fruits, Parmesan cheese, Riviera cheese, fresh almonds on vine leaves, roasted chestnuts, sweetened curds, wafers, ring-molded cakes, fresh stalk fennel, unspecified "sweets and confections"—and *buon apetito*!

Granted, such inventories aren't necessarily translatable as simple gluttony; without further information there's no knowing whether fifty carp were meant to feed as many guests or ten times that number. Still, Lorenzo de' Medici didn't acquire his sobriquet "the Magnificent" by living meanly, nor did Elizabeth of England rot the teeth out of her head by going easy on the sweets. But if a few unbridled appetites incurred the censure of the more puritanical wing of the clergy and if an occasional sumptuary law was enacted in Florence and elsewhere, the characteristics of Renaissance gastronomy in general remained finesse, restraint, balance, and order. And if Renaissance man ate with renewed zest, it was zest born of a renewed interest in all aspects of his humanity and of a moderate, reasoned approach to his manifold affairs. The difference between his gastronomic style and that of both his predecessors and more flamboyant contemporaries might almost be likened to the difference between faithfulness and promiscuity. While the one may generate less high excitement than the other, its rewards tend to be more satisfying in the long run.

MOLVQVES

baie perdue

Coste dangereuse

GRANDE   IAVE

PETITE
IAVE

MER·DE·LINDE ORIENTALE

4

A Spicy Tale

Awake, O north wind; and come, thou south; blow upon my garden, that the spices thereof may flow out.

Song of Solomon 4:16

Evil and strife are endemic to the Moluccas, for the clove, though a creation of God, is actually an apple of discord and responsible for more afflictions than gold.

João de Barros

To THE MODERN WESTERN MIND, preoccupied with the potentially disastrous consequences of an Arab near-monopoly in oil, the historical importance of pepper is almost incomprehensible. It is usually hidden in an obscure corner of the supermarket, and while it makes a pleasant but not overly significant addition to most dishes eaten in the West, its omission from them hardly would be considered a matter of global concern. And if pepper, the most ubiquitous of spices, is of so little interest, could nutmeg, mace, cloves, and cinnamon ever have bestirred the passions of men or brought nations to the brink of war and beyond? They could have and did. Consider this report, delivered by the directors of the English East India Company in the seventeenth century:

> If the present misunderstandings between the two nations [Britain and Holland] should ferment to an open war, it would be thought by the vulgar but a war for pepper which they think to be [a] slight thing. . . . But at the Bottom it will prove a war for the dominion of the British as well as the Indian seas, because if ever [the Dutch] come to be sole masters of that Commodity as they already are of nutmegs, mace, cloves, and cinnamon, the sole profit of that one commodity pepper being of general use, will be more to them, than all the rest and in probability sufficient to defray the constant charge of a great navy in Europe.

Neither polar explorers nor lunar astronauts set out in search of spices, but a great many of their predecessors did. Although he was a general merchant interested in any and all negotiable goods, Marco Polo came home to Venice with eye-popping descriptions of Chinese ginger, Tibetan cloves, and the spicy wonders of Java. ("The country

The search for a sea route to the fabled Spice Islands and other eastern entrepôts sparked an age of exploration and imperialism that was without precedent in all of European history. In the sixteenth-century map of Java and the Moluccas opposite, Europeans barter for spices while one of their number takes time out for some hunting. At upper left, a cargo-laden ship sails for home.

abounds with rich commodities. Pepper, nutmegs, spikenard, galangal, cubebs, cloves and all other valuable spices and drugs, are the produce of the island; which occasion it to be visited by many ships laden with merchandise, that yields to the owners considerable profit.") Always an interested observer of gastronomical customs, Polo also noted that the Tartars ate their meat raw—hence the modern steak tartare, which originally was tenderized by riding with it under the saddle. His interest in spices notwithstanding, however, he neglected to inform the West how this dish was seasoned.

Marco Polo was the first of many spice-motivated explorers. Henry the Navigator's observations and calculations enabled early Portuguese seafarers to return from West Africa with cargoes of pepper. While Bartholomeu Dias fought his way around the Cape of Good Hope in search of an eastward passage to India, still another Portuguese, Pedro de Covilhão, made his way overland to Calicut on India's west coast, whence he relayed to Lisbon briefings on the navigability of the Indian Ocean and, not incidentally, the most promising spice centers on the Malabar Coast. Girolama da Santo, a Genoese trader, also traveled overland to India, but then continued by sea to Ceylon, Sumatra, and the Maldive Islands. Vasco da Gama landed in India "in search of Christians and spices," finding enough of the latter to enable a grateful Portuguese king to one-up his Spanish counterpart by advising him that, "Of these they have brought a great quantity, including cinnamon, cloves, ginger, nutmeg. . . ." Like his more celebrated compatriot Christopher Columbus, the Italian John Cabot (Giovanni Caboto) sailed westward for the Indies and spices. And while he unquestionably believed the landfall he made in June of 1497 was Asia, the place certainly didn't resemble Polo's descriptions and yielded nothing resembling cloves or peppercorns.

And, of course, there was poor Columbus himself, so obsessed with the lure of the gold and spices of the Indies that when a large tract of real estate interposed itself between the admiral and his goal he was able to accomplish nothing more impressive than to call its inhabitants Indians and return more or less empty-handed to a queen who had gone into hock to bankroll his journey. Undaunted, he made further trips to the "Indies," only to bring home syphilitic crews, pineapples that refused to grow in Europe, tales of cinnamon and ginger of whose existence he could produce not a shred of evidence, and a form of "pepper" (actually the pimiento) that can only have been a distinct letdown to backers who expected the genuine article—although it was later to play a prominent role in the Spanish cuisine. But the land he went to his grave believing was spice-rich Hindustan was soon to play a role of no mean significance itself, both in world history and the more circumscribed history of gastronomy.

By the third decade of the sixteenth century the Western European quest for spices had decisively shifted the balance of world power and the focus of world interest. The Spaniards, to be sure, had by then switched their concentration from the peppercorns and nutmeg of the East to the gold, silver, and foodstuffs of the New World—a switch that still affects the nature of Iberian cookery—but spices had

Seventeen-year-old Marco Polo set out for China with his father and uncle in 1271. It was to take the young Venetian merchant four years to reach the court of the Great Khan, and once there Polo (seen above in traditional Tartar attire) was to spend seventeen years in the service of the Mongol emperor. In the words of poet John Masefield, Marco Polo's account of his epochal journey "created Asia for the European mind." The Book of Marvels was filled with descriptions of the wonders of the Orient—and, in particular, the spices that abounded there. The illustration at right, depicting a pepper harvest in southern India, is taken from a fourteenth-century edition of Polo's work.

provided the initial impetus and continued to occupy the interest of the Portuguese and others. To put the ultimate consequences of the spice trade into appreciable perspective, it eventually culminated in the governance by a company of merchants of nearly one-fifth of the world's known population.

The Moslem peoples had long controlled the overland spice routes, with Venetian traders acting as the conduits whereby the pungent stuffs of Asia entered Europe. The conveyance of a cargo of spices from its source to the tables of the West was a tortuous and costly enterprise involving all manner of transportation, middlemen, and extortionate imposts—and it ran wholesale prices up to some eight times what they had been at the point of origin by the time they reached the threshold of Europe. With the capture of Constantinople by the Ottoman Turks in 1453, an already bad situation—at least as far as the West was concerned—took a marked turn for the worse as the Mediterranean and its littoral fell under the effective control of the East. Insofar as spices went, the West found itself in much the same bind as that in which the oil-consuming industrialized nations were to find themselves in 1974. Spices could still be had, but at a cost so prohibitive that only royalty could afford them. The solution to this state of affairs, of course, was to go directly to the source of supply.

In such circumstances those nations that bordered on the Atlantic —until then marginal factors in the international scheme of things— suddenly had power thrust upon them. Navigational advances pioneered by the Portuguese and accelerated by the spice race, as William H. McNeill observes in *The Rise of the West*, were to link Western Europe with the rest of the earth:

> What had always been the extreme fringe of Eurasia became, within little more than a generation, a focus of the world's sea lanes, influencing and being influenced by every human society within easy reach of the sea. Thereby the millennial land-centered balance among the Eurasian civilizations was abruptly challenged and, within three centuries, reversed.

Columbus and Cabot had been both right and wrong. India and the Spice Islands could be reached by sailing westward, but the trip was far more arduous and roundabout than they could have known. As they had since Phoenician times, the spice routes to the Indies remained for the most part easterly, with high-pooped vessels laden with trade goods rounding the South African cape to enter the warm Indian Ocean, where flying fish skittered over the surface and pulses quickened at the heady imminence of peppercorns and mace, cinnamon and cloves, cardamom and nutmeg; where the very air seemed redolent of spices; where Sumatra, Java, Borneo, and the Celebes beckoned from the sea's rim and, beyond them, rode the Moluccas—the fabled Spice Islands.

While Columbus obstinately continued to poke around the Caribbean in search of the Indian mainland, the Portuguese were setting up trade outposts on the east coast of Africa and, by 1505, the year of Columbus's death, had made a landing as far north as Mombasa, a major Arab spice entrepôt. Later they crossed the Indian Ocean to plant trade centers at Ormuz on the Persian Gulf and in Bombay, Calicut, Goa,

The Portuguese were steadfast in their determination to find an eastern sea route to India. Their perseverance was rewarded first with Bartholomeu Dias's momentous journey around the Cape of Good Hope and later with Vasco da Gama's arrival at Calicut in 1498. Portuguese domination of the eastern sea lanes brought prosperous merchants (right) to Portugal's bustling ports. Supremacy in the spice trade passed from the Venetians to the Portuguese, and Lisbon (left) became a vast clearinghouse for pepper, cloves, ginger, mace, and cinnamon. A European view of this last crop being harvested is shown at left, below.

Ceylon, and Malacca. By 1513 they had penetrated as far as Canton on the China coast, and some forty years later—with a secure base nearby at Macao—had established effective control of trade with the Moluccas. Of these islands Francisco Serrão was to write his fellow Portuguese Ferdinand Magellan, saying, "I have discovered yet another New World, greater and richer than Vasco da Gama's." Magellan finally vindicated Columbus by sailing westward in 1519 in the service of Spain "to discover the spice islands in the Indian Ocean, lying in the Spanish half of the world." By the time his battered fleet reached the Moluccas, Magellan himself was dead and the Portuguese were well established there. Spain, by then far too absorbed in divesting American Indians of gold that lay at the end of a much shorter rainbow, ceded her dubious claim to the Moluccas for a cash settlement and to all intents and purposes dropped out of the spice trade. Ironically, Juan Sebastián del Cano, who brought home 77,000 pounds of spices (more than enough to defray the cost of the expedition) and the remnants of Magellan's fleet after an unplanned circumnavigation of the globe, was rewarded with a coat of arms emblazoned with clove branches, nutmeg, and cinnamon.

If Spain had abandoned the spice quest—a defection still felt by non-Spaniards in the pepperless restaurants of Madrid and Barcelona—other nations had not. By the early seventeenth century the Dutch were well established in the easternmost reaches of the Indian Ocean and had made serious inroads against Portuguese supremacy there. Master shipbuilders and redoubtable sailors who had learned to take the worst nature had to offer in the howling fisheries of the North Sea, the Dutch were also Western Europe's greatest traders, bringing to mercantile ventures an enthusiasm utterly repugnant to the visionary Portuguese temperament and playing a large part in the European distribution of Portuguese spices, for which they traded their own preserved fish. After vainly seeking a northern passage to the Indies in an effort to circumvent a blockade imposed by Philip II of Spain, the Dutch boldly took the southern route to the Indian Ocean, which, after considerable bloodshed, the United East India Company ruthlessly was to dominate from its capital, Batavia, on the northwestern coast of Java.

In the waning years of the sixteenth century the English, still flushed with their victory over the Spanish Armada a dozen years earlier and quickened by an emergent capitalism, dealt themselves into the action by forming their own East India Company in hopes of driving down the cost of pepper, which had trebled as the Dutch and Portuguese contended for power in the Indian Ocean. Its charter, signed by an aging Queen Elizabeth who would not live to see the first expedition return with 1,030,000 pounds of pepper, would eventually prove to be a license, in effect, for the formation of the greatest empire the world has ever known. The English, with armed merchantmen bearing such names as *Trade's Increase*, *Merchant Royal*, *Clove*, and *Peppercorn*, never succeeded in breaking the Dutch hold on the spice trade, but the rivalry, spurred by Dutch torture and massacre of English traders in the Moluccas, led to wars that once again changed the political alignment of the globe, eventuating in the exchange of the sugar-rich South American territory of Surinam for New York and diverting the interests of the English to the New World and to India and its tea.

Why this rage for spices, which lasted several centuries? Why, in particular, among peoples whose cuisines later were to be numbered among the least piquant in the world? Why would thousands of men risk scurvy, drowning, or violent death at the hands of brown or other white men in remote corners of the globe, all for a few peppercorns or the dried buds of the evergreen *Eugenia aromatica*? The answer is simple: rank meat.

For centuries domestic animals had brought forth their young in the spring, fattened themselves during the summer, and been slaughtered (except for a few kept for breeding purposes) in the late fall to forestall their starvation during the long fodderless winters. For a short time after the traditional Martinmas slaughter in November, fresh domestic meat was eaten; an annual treat that was extended as long as possible, even to the point of putrescence. For some, of course, game provided fresh meat during the winter, but while a rabbit or thin wild pig could be consumed at a sitting, venison or bear usually couldn't and would keep only for a few days even in cold weather. (The notion, still current, that game is at its best when well hung may easily reflect tastes formed not so much by the palate as by an earlier exigency, and much of the notorious gluttony of the privileged classes during the course of history may simply have represented an attempt to consume food before it spoiled.)

In an age without refrigeration even royalty had to contend with high meat. Indeed, the rich and powerful doubtless had to put up with more rancidity than anyone else, since it was they who were the meat-eaters and it was a rare peasant who could afford the luxury of killing a draft or milk animal for his own consumption. A large proportion of all meat butchered was dried, salted, or smoked for future use, of course,

The scenes of Indian court life that enliven this seventeenth-century cushion cover show the influences of Mogul rule on Indian gastronomy. From the Moguls came dishes of rice and shredded meat, the technique of mixing fruit in meat dishes, the use of almonds and rosewater, and the delights of sugar candy.

but while such curing processes inhibited decay they couldn't postpone it indefinitely and as winter wore on molds formed, meats spoiled faster than they could be eaten, and the resultant stench could have done little to sharpen the appetite.

Spices and other aromatic agents had been used both as preservatives and for their cosmetic effect on decaying foods since ancient times. The Egyptians had flavored—or disguised the flavor of—their meats with cinnamon (which grew nowhere in or near Egypt) as early as 1450 B.C., and the Phoenicians were familiar with many Far Eastern spices. The liberal Greek use of asafetida may have been an instance of fighting fire with fire, and Alaric the Visigoth esteemed pepper highly enough to exact tribute from the Romans that included 30,000 pounds of it—a staggering quantity considered in terms of the population at that time.

In the classical era cassia, or Chinese cinnamon, was sent westward via the silk route. True East Indian cinnamon, a milder product, made its way to the Mediterranean regions from the Indonesian archipelago, the Malay peninsula, and Ceylon either aboard lateen-rigged cargo vessels that hugged the southern coasts of Asia or by outrigger canoes that audaciously crossed the open sea to Madagascar and the east coast of Africa. Mace, nutmeg, and cloves also came from Indonesia, camphor from Borneo, cardamom from Malaya, ginger from the China and Malabar coasts, asafetida from Persia, frankincense from Arabia. For the most part these commodities were conveyed by Arab traders who were at some pains to keep their customers in the dark concerning the whereabouts of their sources.

This was the situation, unchanged in its essentials, for hundreds of years. In the fifteenth century, however, with the takeover by the Ottoman Turks of key trade junctures previously under the control of the Mongols, it deteriorated markedly, at least insofar as all Europeans were concerned save the Venetians and Florentines, who still maintained a piece of the action. With that deterioration came the big chance of the nations bordering on the Atlantic.

In a sense the more celebrated gluttons of the sixteenth and seven-

Elizabeth Blackwell's A Curious Herbal, *published in 1739, illustrates some of the spices that lured European traders eastward. In an age without refrigeration, Guinea pepper (far left), Java cinnamon (left), and Malaysian cardamom (above) were used primarily to mask the flavor of rank meat. But spices were by no means the East's sole contribution to European gastronomy. The Saracens introduced Westerners to sherbet, flake pastry, and cane sugar as well as to the orange (above, right).*

teenth centuries might be said to have fattened themselves on spices, for without massive admixtures of cloves, ginger, mace, pepper, cinnamon, and the like they could hardly have choked their meals down and might have been, if not precisely cadaverous, at least fashionably svelte. One modern writer, Reay Tannahill, disagrees with this view, arguing that the medieval use of spices was not nearly as prodigal as impractical observers ("these learned gentlemen are no cooks") would have us believe. In support of her thesis she cites a fish stew recipe from the single medieval cookbook, by "the Goodman of Paris," that made a systematic attempt to quantify its ingredients. The recipe calls for some fifty pounds of assorted fish, ½ oz. saffron, 2 oz. "small spices," ¼ lb. cinnamon, and ½ lb. ginger. Now, fifty pounds is a lot of fish, but nearly a pound is an *awful* lot of spices, and were a modern chef to concoct a *bouillabaisse* with proportionate amounts of seasoning he'd find himself out of a job. Moreover, fish was generally fresher than meat in the Middle Ages and didn't require the excessively liberal dosages of aromatics that rancid flesh demanded.

Prodigious quantitites of spices were imported into Europe and, since they were far beyond the means of the common man (who made do with garlic, onions, leeks, and the more familiar aromatic herbs), they can only have been used with stupefying prodigality at the tables of the rich. The recipe for "Chekyn for a Lorde," for example, which appeared in *The Forme of Cury,* a cookbook written sometime during the reign of Richard II, advises its readers to "Take checones and make hom clene, and chop hom on quarters, and sethe hom, and when these byn half sethen take hom up and pylle of[f] the skynne, and fry hom in fair grese and dress hom up, and cast thereon pouder of gynger and sugur; then take iii pounds of almondes, and blanche hom, and draw up a good thik mylke with the brothe, and other good brothe

therewith, and do hit in a pot and sethe hit; and put thereunto hole clowes, maces and pynes, and let hit boyle altogedur, and in the setting down do thereto an ounce of pouder of gynger, and medal [muddle] it with vyngar, and serve hit forth, and pour the syrip thereon, and coast [cast] thereon a pouder of gynger and sugur; and a hole chekyn for a Lorde." A hole chekyn, it might be added, for a Lorde with a sweet tooth and an anesthetized palate.

Spices, however, were by no means the East's sole contribution to European gastronomy. As has been noted, the Romans imported culinary exotica from everywhere in the known world (with particular emphasis on Asia Minor), the Saracens introduced many of their foods and foodstuffs to the West and much of the bounty brought home by the Crusaders took edible form. The juice of the bigarade, or bitter orange, long had been used in the West to camouflage the less agreeable aspects of corrupted meat, but the true orange whose name derives from the Sanskrit *nāranga* and remains almost unchanged in various European languages, notably the Spanish (*naranja*), was brought westward by the Saracens. As has been mentioned earlier, the Saracens also brought sherbet and flake pastry to Europe and were directly or indirectly responsible for the introduction there of lemons, cane sugar, spinach, marzipan, and buckwheat (still "Saracen" in the Romance languages). From them, the Crusaders also took pomegranates, apricots, tarragon, mint, and the technique for distilling *al-kuhul*.

Just as the Western Europeans later were to contend with the Arabs and Turks for dominance of the trade routes and to circumvent Arab blockades, so had the Arabs vied with Byzantium for centuries, and so had they been forced to circumvent a Byzantine blockade by moving their capital from Damascus to Baghdad, which became the great clearinghouse for Asian trade and, like Rome before it, a synonym for sybaritic gastronomy. Nobles in the court of a tenth-century caliph were expected to deliver learned disquisitions on the culinary arts, poets composed menus in verse, and princes of the blood wrote cookbooks. Pork, blood, and wine were proscribed, but not much else. Most of what was eaten—meats, fruits, nuts, and vegetables—was cooked together in a single pot (a natural outgrowth of the Bedouin life-style) and meat was ingested in quantities unheard of in Europe (another legacy of the nomadic existence in which the only practical way to deal with slaughtered meat was to consume it on the spot).

As was the case with other cuisines, the tides of conquest and political change had their effects on Arabic cookery, which was heavily influenced first by the Persians, who developed a sophisticated rice-based cuisine a thousand years ago (and whose first king they credited with the invention of cooking), and later by the Mongols. From the Persians, with their abundance of melons, lemons, pomegranates,

peaches, and apricots, the Arabs derived the customs of cutting fatty mutton with fruits and fruit juices and of thickening pot liquors with the flour of almonds, pistachios, and walnuts. From their own fat-tailed sheep came the basic oil of Arab cookery, and chopped meat—a substance at least as vital to present-day American existence as television and petroleum—seems to have been an Arabic invention.

The Arabs contributed enormously to the sciences but little to the arts of the West and, gastronomically speaking, provided the world at large with more ingredients than dishes. One contribution that had an incalculable impact, however, was coffee, the "wine of Islam." According to legend the beverage was discovered in Ethiopia in the ninth century when a goatherd noticed that his charges were getting high on the berries of the tree now known as *Coffea arabica*. Lacking the digestive system of a goat, the man tried boiling some of the fruit, drank off the resultant decoction and found that it produced a state of mild euphoria and a concomitant case of insomnia. How the fun-loving goatherd contrived to while away long nights remains a matter of conjecture.

The stimulant caught on sometime later in southern Arabia, where around the turn of the fifteenth century it was discovered that roasting and grinding the berries resulted in an even better drink. Coffee filtered (or, perhaps, percolated?) into Turkey by the middle of the sixteenth

century and may have reached Western Europe somewhat earlier. By 1650, in any case, the first European coffeehouse had opened in Oxford and within two decades similar establishments began appearing in France, Italy (where coffee is still prepared and drunk more or less in the Arab manner), and elsewhere. Then, in 1683, an enterprising Viennese named Kolschitzky, who supposedly had encountered the fragrant bean when it was left behind during the Turkish siege of Vienna, opened that city's first café. If the Turks had failed to take Vienna, their abandoned beverage did—by storm—and it was there that the Western custom of adding cream to the drink was initiated. The Near Eastern coffee monopoly was broken in the eighteenth century by Dutch entrepreneurs who found that the caffeinated bean could be grown in one of their East Indian possessions, Java. Later, of course, South America would become the world's major supplier.

Deprived of any significant share of the spice trade, the British developed their own interests, particularly in India. Salient among these was tea, which had been known in Holland and Portugal by around 1610 and which reached England and France a couple of decades later. (Members of the Russian court drank Chinese tea at about the same time, but it was not to be until the nineteenth century that tea would become the Russian national beverage and the steaming samovar the very symbol of Russian life.) Although its initial appearance in England had led some bemused hostesses to serve tea leaves on bread—a misunderstanding later repeated in New England—tea had by 1770 largely replaced beer and coffee as the great British drink and, inevitably, was being denounced in some quarters as a source of unspeakable perversions, as socially destructive as gin. At the other extreme some Englishmen, like many Chinese, considered it the universal panacea. By then, the English were consuming 18,000,000 pounds of tea annually and apparently enjoying every cupful. In the American colonies, though, oppressive tea taxes invested the beverage with an increasingly bitter flavor. The colonists vented their anger by hosting the Boston Tea Party of 1773, and the early association of tea with oppression and "taxation without representation" may be partly responsible for turning the United States into a nation of coffee drinkers.

5

The New World's Bounty

Who ever heard of the Indian Peru?
Or who in venturous vessel measured
The Amazons' huge river, now found true?
Or fruitfullest Virginia, who did ever view?

Yet all these were when no man did them know;
Yet have from wisest ages hidden been;
And later times things more unknown shall show.

Edmund Spenser

IN HIS UNDERSTANDABLE ENTHUSIASM for the wonders of a "new-found-land" Spenser seems to have confused a species with a nationality. By "no man" he meant no Englishman, or at the very least no European. By the time the stay-at-home poet's more venturesome compatriots made their belated attempts to establish a foothold in the Western Hemisphere, however, the Indians of the Americas had been in residence for quite some time. And long, long before Spenser's remote ancestors had stopped painting themselves blue the indigenous peoples of the New World had sensed that their soil was, as Sir Walter Ralegh was to write of Virginia's, "the most plentiful, sweet, fruitful and wholesome of all the world."

The European access to the East that opened up in the sixteenth century had produced a handful of foods previously unknown in Europe: tea, coffee, the coconut, the banana, the mango. For the most part, though, its gastronomical significance lay in its having made more readily available foodstuffs that had been known in the West for centuries. The discovery of America was an altogether different story. From the moment that Columbus was presented by the Indians of Haiti with a gift of sweet potatoes, early voyagers to the New World were to be treated to an incredible succession of edibles that were entirely new to them; foods whose cultural, economic, and political impact on European life were to be incalculable; foods that would, as new foods had since time immemorial, change the customs of peoples—and in this case the face of lands that lay half a world away. And whereas travelers like Ralph Lane, who sailed with Grenville in 1584 to set up an English colony on Roanoke Island, saw the New World as potentially affording a larger, more bountiful extension of life much as it was lived in their

Theodor de Bry's 1590 engraving opposite depicts the American Indian village of Secotan in what later became North Carolina. At right, fields of corn have been sown at carefully timed intervals and are in distinctly different stages of development. Also to be seen are a pumpkin garden (I), a ceremonial feast (D), a ritual dance (C), and a deer hunt (upper left).

own countries ("If Virginia had but horses and kine in some reasonable proportion, I dare assure myself, being inhabited by English no realm in Christendom were comparable to it."), Stephen Vincent Benét, with the benefit of two and a half centuries of hindsight, saw the situation more clearly:

> And those who came were resolved
>   to be Englishmen
> Gone to the world's end,
>   but English every one,
> And they ate the white corn-kernels,
>   parched in the sun,
> And they knew it not,
>   but they'd not be English again.

The poet John Donne, for whom the New World provided an extraordinary metaphor for an amorous conquest ("O my America!" he addressed a new mistress, "my new-found-land"), described the hemisphere he would never see as:

> That unripe side of earth, that heavy clime
> That gives us man up now, like Adam's time
> Before he ate. . . .

A pretty conceit, but the fact is that the hungry innocent Donne celebrated so rhapsodically had been eating—and eating very well indeed, thank you—for a good long time. Among other things he had been eating corn, or maize, a grain Columbus found "most tasty, boiled, roasted or ground into flour." Corn had probably originated in the southern Mexican highlands as a wild grass, much as wheat had in the Old World before the onset of the Neolithic revolution. Over the centuries the Indians had domesticated it, discovering in the process that it grew best when planted in small circular hummocks spaced in rows a yard or so apart. They also discovered that it prospered particularly well when a fish—a nitrogen-rich fertilizer as men were later to learn—was buried in each hummock as an offering to the gods. As described by Thomas Mariot, the first Englishman to write of the grain, its kernels were "of divers colors" and yielded a "very white and sweet flowre" and "as good ale as was to bee desired."

Corn meal had been eaten in pre-Columbian Mexico as a breakfast dish and as the twice-cooked staple flatbread the Conquistadors were to call the *tortilla* (an altogether different affair from the omelets of the same name eaten in Spain) and that remains the universal Mexican bread and basis, moist or dry, warmed or cold, for such preparations as *tostadas, nachos, tacos, enchiladas,* and *tamales* (not only corn meal but corn husks figure in the latter, which are made by stuffing a *tortilla* with a combination of beans, tomatoes, and meat, fish, or fowl and steaming it in the husks). North of the Rio Grande, Indians steamed or boiled whole ears of fresh ripe corn, used the kernels in *misickquatash* (succotash) or pounded them in a mortar to produce such breads as ashcakes and pone, and cereals like *rockahominy* (whence hominy) and samp, which was sweetened with wild honey or maple syrup and

Much as Prometheus gave fire to the Greeks, so, according to an ancient Aztec legend, the god Quetzalcoatl gave corn to early Mesoamerican man. The grain's importance cannot be over-emphasized, for corn became the staff of life in Mesoamerica—and as such was depicted in numerous artworks of the pre-Columbian period. At left is a representation of the Zapotec corn god; he wears a maize headdress and a loincloth of husks. Above, a Colima dog fetches a somewhat undersized ear of corn; below, a Colima woman grinds corn kernels into meal using a device known as a metate. The ground meal is then shaped into tortillas—one of which is about to be sampled by the mischievous child at the woman's left.

which is still sold along the roadside near eastern Long Island's Shinnecock reservation at harvest time.

The list of the Western Hemisphere's contributions to world gastronomy is almost endless. To the Indians of the Americas the Italian owes the zucchini he has made so much his own that it's now called Italian squash in many parts of its homeland; the Spaniard his pimiento, his *gazpacho Andaluz*, his *chorizo* sausage, and many of his favorite beans; the Hungarian his paprika; the Hawaiian his pineapple; the African his peanuts (a staple crop in many regions). Had the New World gone undiscovered Frenchmen today would not be eating *ratatouille*, the popular Provençal vegetable mélange, half of whose components are of American origin. Nor would they be eating turkey, which Brillat-Savarin described as the most savory of domestic fowl and "one of the handsomest presents which the New World has offered to the Old"; nor even *haricots verts*, so emblematic of Gallic cookery that Americans have come to call them French beans. Had the Western Hemisphere been left undisturbed India, Malaysia, and southeastern China never would have known the chili peppers that add so much pizzazz to their cuisines, the Swiss couldn't have invented milk chocolate, *bouillabaisse* would be just another fish chowder, Cinderella's coach might have been turned into a cabbage or a watermelon, Peter of the nursery rhyme might have stuffed an eggplant with his faithless wife, and English letters would have been spared the embarrassment of essayist Sidney Smith's line, "Ah, you flavor everything; you are the vanilla of society."

For various reasons not all the foods known to the Indians were to enjoy widespread popularity in the Old World. In some cases they simply weren't exportable. In others, they were too difficult to raise in alien soil, couldn't break through entrenched tradition (many peoples are particularly reluctant to change their staple grains no matter how beneficial a change might be), were falsely believed to be poisonous, or were just plain repugnant to European sensibilities.

Delicious as they may be, the Brazil nut, black walnut, and cashew have played negligible roles in European gastronomy—and the wild blueberry of coastal New England, none at all. The avocado, from which the Yucatán Indians made—and all Mexicans still make—their *guacamole*, is little known in Europe and the acorn squash even less so. The American persimmon (which John Smith found "will draw a mans mouth awrie" when eaten green but was comparable to the apricot when ripe) is overlooked by the usually reliable *Larousse Gastronomique*, which limits its comment to the Asian variety; and the impact on the Old World of the papaya (a source of commercial meat tenderizers with which the persimmon is often confused) has been less than seismic. Manioc, or cassava, the staple grain of much of South America, enjoyed a brief vogue in France and Spain but today is known to most Europeans only through a by-product, tapioca. If these and other New World foods—among them the oppossum, raccoon, quahog, softshelled clam, moose, turtle (and its eggs), and all manner of berries—weren't exported, they were avidly eaten *in situ* by the new arrivals. And they would continue to be eaten by their descendants, whose diets

would never be English—or Spanish, Dutch, French, or whatever they had been—again.

Of all those cornucopian wonders—and what a cornucopia Columbus had stumbled on!—nurtured by the sweet soil of another world, two in particular were to revolutionize Old World gastronomy. A third was, for better or worse, to provide mankind with an altogether unprecedented sensory experience.

Humble though it may be, the common potato is indispensable to life as it is lived in much of the Western world. Far and away the most versatile and least demanding of foodstuffs, it is receptive to every known cooking process. There is no shape, form, or texture to which it won't adapt itself, no category of savor in which it can't easily be included. It is the most convivial of all foods and the most gregarious. Transcending all social classifications, it comforts the peasantry, delights the aristocracy, and nourishes them both. No less acceptable to the most esoteric gourmet than to the most brutalized laborer, its guises are inexhaustibly multifarious. Of all man's foods it is the most difficult to cook badly and, no matter what it is served with, the least likely to be mismatched. But it wasn't always so highly regarded.

A widespread belief to the contrary notwithstanding, the potato is not native to North America and in fact seems to have made its way there from England. It was shipped to England from Colombia in 1568, a couple of decades after the Spaniards there had imported it from Peru. The tuber was casually being eaten in Italy by the turn of the seventeenth century, but encountered surprising resistance elsewhere on the Continent. In many parts of France, for example (a country where life without the potato would be almost inconceivable today and where well over a hundred standardized recipes, exclusive of soups, are in extensive use), it was thought to induce leprosy, of all things. The Swiss, notable consumers famed today for their *rösti* potatoes, shunned it for fear of scrofula, and the Prussians, who put away their share and more these days, flatly refused to eat potatoes brought in to provide famine relief as late as 1774. The reasons for this unwonted timidity aren't easy to come by. It might be noted, however, that although it is one of the most benign of foods the potato, like the eggplant, belongs to the botanical family that numbers belladonna, or deadly nightshade, and henbane (of which Hamlet's father got a fatal earful) among its less savory members.

Despite its slow start, the eventual conversion of Europeans to the potato was to have profound and lasting effects on the social, economic, cultural, and political fortunes of the Western world. In time it would have disastrous consequences in Ireland and elsewhere and radically alter the ethnic makeup of the American population.

The tomato, too, met with resistance in the Old World. The Italians, who have devoted a considerable part of their energies to its glorification, were growing it in their own country by around the middle of the sixteenth century, but only as a decorative plant they called *pomo*

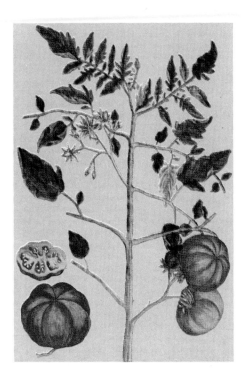

Jacques le Moyne accompanied a French expedition to Florida in 1564 and in a later painting (from which Theodor de Bry made the engraving at left) attempted to portray the New World's bounty. Indians are shown in supplication around a pillar, at the base of which are arranged corn, squash, and other native comestibles. Not shown but also included in the cornucopia of new foods that Columbus stumbled upon were lima, kidney, and navy beans, vanilla and chocolate, and both the potato and the tomato (right).

d'oro, or "apple of gold." (Unfamiliar produce of more or less spherical shape, incidentally, has had a history of being called "apples" of one description or another. The French, always ready to put an amorous construction on matters and convinced that theirs is the only language worth speaking, heard "*pomo d'oro*" as "*pomme d'amour*" and at first called the tomato "apple of love.") Imported from Mexico, where it was called *tomatl* by the Aztecs and *manzana* ("apple" again) by the Spaniards, the fruit of *Lycopersicon esculentum*, another member of the nightshade family, was then about the size of the modern cherry tomato and bright yellow. It took the Italians two centuries to get around to eating it; other Europeans were even more circumspect.

In pre-Columbian Mexico and Peru, where the tomato seems to have made an early appearance as a cornfield weed, the Indians had cultivated and eaten it for centuries, making sauces of tomatoes and chili peppers and serving them in stews and as *tamale* fillers. Curiously, however, North American colonists made the acquaintance of the tomato as they had the potato, on the rebound, when it was sent back from the Old World to the New, where its culinary potential was and continues to be left largely uninvestigated, and where it has been rendered almost tasteless and invested with the texture of styrofoam by recent agricultural "improvements."

It was the Italians, once they got going, who recognized the tomato for what it really was: an art form. From those first undersized and probably not very succulent apples of gold they developed the full, red plum tomato, a breed destined as surely to end up in sauce as the Portuguese sardine was to be anointed with oil. By some unfathomable process the Italian and the tomato established a rapport and generated a passion such as most men can't establish with their wives or feel for their mistresses, a oneness such as saints fail to achieve with their gods.

If Europeans were slow to recognize the virtues of the potato and tomato, they lost little time in availing themselves of the dubious benefits of tobacco, even though it, too, belonged to the nightshade family. The first English report of its use dates from John Hawkins's second voyage to the West Indies in 1565, but Columbus's sailors had found Indians smoking it in 1492, and in 1519 Spaniards saw vast fields cultivated by indigenous Mexicans, who mixed aromatics with its leaves in the belief that puffing the weed would cure bronchitis, asthma, and rheumatism. The Spaniards themselves put it under cultivation in Haiti before 1535 and soon thereafter throughout their West Indian colonies and in Venezuela and Brazil, building up a burgeoning trade before the English settlement of Jamestown in 1607.

Sir Walter Ralegh, who brought the potato to Ireland, was responsible for tobacco's introduction into England and its widespread acceptance at court during the last years of Elizabeth's reign, when it was thought to have various medicinal properties. Some forty years earlier, however, the Frenchman André Thevet, who had seen Brazilian Indians smoking cigars wrapped in corn and palm leaves, brought tobacco seed to France, where it was grown in Europe for the first time. Another Frenchman, Jean Nicot, appears to have been the Johnny Appleseed of the plant that later would be assigned to genus *Nicotiana* and make his

name more generally known in the word "nicotine." As French ambassador to the court of Portugal he brought packets of tobacco seed to that country, which soon put them under cultivation. Spain followed suit almost immediately and before long the Belgians, Dutch, and Italians were growing the plant at home with varying degrees of success. By the early seventeenth century it was being grown in Persia and as far afield as India.

Except for the Turks, the peoples of the Old World weren't overly successful as tobacco growers and it was the English colonists in Virginia who soon dominated the European market, shipping their produce to England, whence it was distributed through the Dutch ports. John Rolfe had begun raising "sotweed" at Jamestown in 1612, from South American or West Indian seed, and by 1619 Virginia was sending 20,000 pounds a year eastward across the Atlantic. Later, the colonists learned their crops would produce a much greater yield inland than along the Tidewater and by 1700 were exporting 18,000,000 pounds, a figure that would rise to 40,000,000 by mid-century and 100,000,000 by the outbreak of the Revolution.

Not everyone was caught up in the tobacco craze. James I harbored as abiding a hatred for the pernicious weed as he did for its original importer. "It seems a miracle to me," he groused, "how a custom springing from so vile a ground [ground Ralegh had called the "most wholesome of all the world"] and brought in by a father [the selfsame Ralegh] so generally hated should be welcomed upon so slender a warrant." Robert Burton, author of *The Anatomy of Melancholy*, came on with the good news first, then gave his readers the bad:

> Tobacco, divine, rare, superexcellent tobacco, which goes far beyond all the panaceas, potable gold, and philosopher's stones, a sovereign remedy to all diseases . . . but as it is commonly abused by most men, which take it as tinkers do ale, 'tis a plague, a mischief, a violent purger of goods, lands, health, hellish, devilish and damned tobacco, the ruin and overthrow of body and soul.

While the tomato and the potato were initially greeted with trepidation, Europeans had no such reservations regarding tobacco. Sir Walter Ralegh was responsible for the weed's introduction into England, and André Thevet played a similar role in France. In short order, tobacco reached the rest of Europe, and by the early seventeenth century it was being grown in Persia and as far afield as India (a nabob smoking a hookah is shown above). A detail from the earliest known illustration of an American tobacco factory (left) shows leaves being torn apart (2), twisted (3), and rolled (4). Other leaves are left to dry on the shed's roof. The engraving (right) depicts tobacco sorting and storage processes.

Prom Lupi.

Portus Regalis, fiue F. S. Helenæ.

More recently, the U.S. Surgeon General and several of his more distinguished confreres have delivered themselves of similar animadversions. Their advice has fallen mostly on deaf ears.

Tobacco, it need hardly be said, is in no sense a food and usually is given only negative attention by writers on gastronomy, who tend to condemn it on aesthetic grounds ("Speaking only from the point of view of those who enjoy the pleasures of the table," *Larousse Gastronomique* tells us, ". . . smoking before a meal dulls the sense of taste"). As marginal as tobacco may be to the art of eating, however, that art —and civilized life on earth—might have taken a much different shape had the early settlers planted Virginia with some other cash crop.

Men might smoke but they also had to eat. By and large, the American colonists ate very well indeed; a lot better, it would seem, than most Americans, whatever their means, eat today. Mistakes were made, of course. The boiled young shoots of the Jimsonweed, rampant in Tidewater Virginia, turned those who ate them into "natural Fools" for several days, much as Columbus's men had been driven half-mad by sampling the toxic fruit of the manzanillo tree. As has been noted, an unripe persimmon momentarily dampened John Smith's enthusiasm for the New World's riches, and others had similar misfortunes with strange fruits and unfamiliar greens. And there were larger problems.

America's bounty included exotic fish and animals as well as fruits and vegetables. Indeed, few foods caught the fancy of Europeans as did the native turkey. The bird was brought to Spain in 1511 (at left, Spanish ships are shown entering an American port where outsized turkeys abound), and from there, turkey-raising was to spread through Europe. In the engraving at right, Theodor de Bry has emphasized America's unusual sea life, including a turtle, a manta ray, and two horseshoe crabs.

Michael Drayton, a poet with the soul of an advertising copywriter for General Foods, hymned "Virginia, earth's only Paradise" as a carefree land "Where nature hath in store/Fowle, Venison and Fish/And the Fruitfullest Soyle, Without your toyle . . ." The fact, though, was that earth's only paradise was giving nothing away for nothing but demanded a fair day's work for whatever it yielded; a condition that led many to the brink of starvation. Still, when the colonists learned how to live, they lived quite well.

Plymouth Colony was a case in point. Without Indian guidance the Pilgrims would have starved in a benighted attempt to transfer English life to a very un-English environment. Even with it they barely got through their first year, losing everything they had planted with English seed, harvesting only the corn that Squanto, a compassionate, well-traveled, English-speaking Indian, taught them to cultivate properly, and supplementing a subsistence diet with the game and fish—they themselves were incredibly inept fishermen—he taught them to catch. Even with Squanto's help their first harvest was a modest one. Without it, the experience would have been an unmitigated disaster.

In late November of 1621, Governor William Bradford invited his constituency and their Indian neighbors to the meetinghouse for a little brunch (the first Thanksgiving feast was scheduled to start at 9

77

A.M. and end before noon), a meal at which its participants might, as one of them, Edward Winslow, put it, "after a more speciall manner rejoyce together." Rejoyce they did, for two and a half days longer than had been planned, gorging themselves on ducks, geese and other waterfowl, venison (five freshly bagged deer were contributed by braves in the party of the guest of honor, Massasoit, who was head of the Wampanoag confederacy that ruled southeastern New England), clams, eels, Indian-derived corn breads, and dried wild fruits and berries. According to one scholar's recent findings, the menu did not include turkey.

With one significant exception, little by way of foodstuffs was sent to Europe from colonial America, whose principal trade exports were tobacco and furs. The exception was the great catches of fish, sent dried and salted across the Atlantic from Nova Scotia and Newfoundland (where, incidentally, the word "chowder" probably originated as English crews fed themselves on fish stews similar to those their French rivals enjoyed as *chaudrées* and cooked in pots they called *chaudières*). Otherwise the colonists consumed what they raised, shot, gathered, or caught. And despite Talleyrand's later allegation that Americans had "thirty-two religions but only one dish," they enjoyed an impressively wide range of good things to eat.

New Englanders, for example, had seafood in abundance. One seventeenth-century report enumerated more than two hundred varieties of fish, while another spoke of "such multitudes of sea bass that it seemed . . . one might goe over their backs dri-shod." A third writer described lobsters weighing up to twenty-five pounds and so accessible that "the least boy in the plantation may catch and eat what he will of

While European writers hymned the praises of "fruitfullest Virginia" (title page below, right), the fact of the matter was that the American soil yielded little without a fair share of toil on the part of the early settlers. At Jamestown, and later at Plymouth, the colonists would not have survived without the aid and expertise of the native Americans. The Indians taught them the intertillage system of farming, with single seeds carefully planted (above, right), that was vastly superior to the European method of scattering seed at random. They also introduced the colonists to imaginative ways of preparing the produce from their fields (below, left); corn, for example, was often boiled and eaten directly off the cob.

G · VEEN

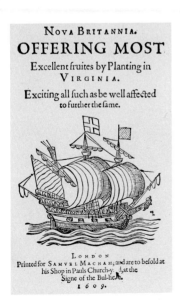

them." Cod was graded as "marchantable, middling, and refuse" and, in that order, exported to Catholic Europe, consumed at home, and sold (under the name "Jamaica fish") to slaveowners in the West Indies. Until well along in the eighteenth century salmon and shad, so highly regarded—and priced—today, were so common around Boston as to be infra dig, with salmon selling for a penny a pound when there were any takers and moving prospective hired hands to stipulate as a condition of employment that they not have to eat it more than once a week. Farther down the seaboard six-foot-long lobsters were caught in New York Bay and foot-long "Gowanes" oysters were plentiful in Brooklyn, where one big-mouthed Dutch traveler remarked that "roasted or stewed [they] make a good bite." Virginia's oysters were said to be even bigger, and its freshwater streams so clotted with fish that they could be beaten to death with sticks or, in some cases, even trodden to death. Terrapin abounded and were highly esteemed, but sturgeon—prohibitively priced today—couldn't be given away.

They had maple sap and its sugar in New England, wild honey almost everywhere. Red and fallow deer ran in herds of hundreds and in 1695 New Yorkers could buy quarters of venison for nine pence; cheap, but more than the price of the whole animal, hide and all, sixty years earlier in Georgia, where a thirty- or forty-pound turkey sold for four pence. Game birds of every kind were a drug on the market, particularly the now-extinct passenger pigeon, which blackened skies for hours on end on its migratory flights and cost a penny a dozen in Boston. Squirrels were not only good eating but so numerous—and so destructive of crops—that a bounty of three pence per head provided

Pennsylvania marksmen with the cash they needed for the few "boughten" things they used. In parts of Virginia, John Smith wrote, "were found some Chestnuts whose wild fruit equalize the best in France, Spaine, Germany, or Italy, to their tastes that had tasted them all." (The native chestnut, *Castanea dentata*, long a staple of American gastronomy, was wiped out in the twentieth century by a fungus disease imported from Japan.)

Not all the New World's bounty was of native origin. Various European fruits, vegetables, and grains, along with cattle, sheep, and swine—and, of course, that incomparable piece of farm machinery, the horse—had to be imported. But once the colonists learned to adapt their methods to local growing conditions these, too, prospered, adding to an already prodigious larder. And from all this plenty the newcomers forged a cuisine; a polyglot cuisine to be sure, a cuisine that combined elements of their various heritages with the traditional cookery of the Indian and included distant echoes of black Africa; a cuisine made up of distinctly recognizable regional subdivisions, but subdivisions that, despite English, Scotch, Irish, French, German, Dutch, Moravian, or

As is evident in the 1853 anony-
mous American primitive painting opposite, apple mead-making
in rural Pennsylvania was more
of a social occasion than anything else. While a few of the
guests are at work paring and
boiling apples, the remainder
dance to the music of local mu-
sicians or imbibe the high-pow-
ered beverage that prompted the
party. That apple mead could be
highly potent is apparent from
the celebrant at center, who is
being carried off by two of his
drinking companions.

African roots, were incontestably American and instantly recognizable as such. Jefferson, America's first great epicure, might smuggle rice out of Italy after experiencing *risotto* there, or serve pasta at the White House; others might bring dishes from other sources. But whatever was imported became naturalized, undergoing sometimes subtle, sometimes startling changes—but never remaining quite what it had been.

Despite the resistance of their women to cornmeal—and it was fierce—the Louisana French learned to eat hominy pudding and to accept Mexican, Spanish, and African influences that gradually transformed their *cuisine Française* into the delicious hybrid known as Creole cooking. The Pennsylvania Dutch added corn chowder to their culinary repertory and continued to bake the *koekjes* of their homeland, thereby ousting the English "biscuit" from the American vocabulary, where it was replaced by "cookie," even as their cabbage (*kool*) salad (*sla*) became not only an American term but a thoroughly American dish as well. Even after the break with England, George Washington would continue to dine on "the King's soup" (a concoction of onions, milk, and egg yolks, spiced with mace and garnished with croutons) and eat Yorkshire pudding with the beef he could hardly chew, but he might enjoy candied sweet potatoes or baked acorn squash at the same meal, finishing up with Indian pudding. Homesick colonists might honor their English origins by baking apple pies, but somehow, somewhere along the way, the dish underwent a sea change, becoming transformed into something ineluctably, emblematically American, just as the hot dog and hamburger, both of German derivation, would much later on.

And they devised a nomenclature for what they ate, anglicizing foreign terms to come up with such names as "jambalaya" (from the Spanish *jamon* and/or French *jambon*), "pone" and "spoon bread" (from the *appone* and *suppawn* of the Indians), "gumbo" (of African dialect derivation), and the like. In other cases the names they used were simplified, speeded-up versions of earlier terms (e.g., "johnny-cake," which comes, depending on which authority you choose to believe, either from "Shawnee cake" or the "journey cake" supposedly so-called because it traveled well). Often they were simply exuberant improvisations, relished for their nonsensicality and born of family jokes or household accidents. But whatever their sources, they entered the language, adding to it much the same savor that the dishes themselves added to life, investing both with a folk poetry made up of hush puppies and burgoo, shoo-fly pie and apple pandowdy, tangle breeches and cinnamon flop, berry grunt and apple slump, hopping john and sticky bun, snickerdoodles, kinkawoodles, graham jakes, and thus back to johnny-cakes.

In a few short years precarious settlements had weathered the privations of the bitter first winters and were joyously reaping the bounty of the Promised Land. "With their miseries," wrote William Bradford, the first governor of Plymouth Colony, of his constituents, "they opened a way to these new lands; and after these stormes, with what ease other men came to inhabite in them . . . so as to seem to goe to a bride feaste wher all things are provided for them."

6

The French Touch

Vatel's death is the greatest event in the whole history of cookery since Prometheus stole fire from heaven. When the mythic hero stole that fire from the gods, he made cookery possible; when Vatel stabbed himself in the royal castle of Chantilly, he at once and forever vindicated for cookery its position among the noble arts.

E. S. Dallas
Kettner's Book of the Table

THE VATEL IN QUESTION, the rest of whose name is unknown, was not a chef as is generally supposed but a *maître d'hotel* and master carver in the service of Louis XIV. The incident at Chantilly is supposed to have occurred in 1671 when, mortified beyond endurance by the nondelivery of a couple of roasts and a basket of fish, the hapless fellow is said to have declaimed, "I have lost my fame. I cannot bear this disgrace!" and put an end to his suffering. Given his fastidious professionalism ("A carver," he wrote, ". . . should make his obeisance when approaching the table, proceed to carve the viands, and divide them understandingly"), one can almost imagine him pausing at the fatal moment to consider which of his knives was the correct one for the job.

Vatel wasn't the only figure in French gastronomy to take such extreme measures. Just a few years ago the downgrading by the *Guide Michelin* of one restaurant precipitated the suicide of the chef, and one never knows when a collapsed soufflé or scorched *gigot* will impel its distraught author to orphan his children and widow his wife.

The French take their food seriously. They have evolved a gastronomical and oenological vocabulary more inclusive and more finely shaded than that of any other Western language, replete with terms— even gestures—that have no ready equivalents elsewhere. There is no single English word for *apéritif*, for example, and even the clumsy compound "before-dinner drink" altogether misses the point. There are no words, either, for *primeurs* (the first spring vegetables), *darne* (a large slice of fish), *macédoine* (a mixture of early vegetables or fruits), *crudités* (raw vegetables), *poelé* (butter-roasted), *amourettes* (the spinal marrow of oxen and calves), *suprême* (boned breast of fowl), *pluches* (the leaves of certain plants, such as chervil), *noisette* (the center or "eye" of a chop), or *charcuterie* (the German "delicatessen" is the best we've got), while to translate *dégustation* as "tasting" is about as

That the French take their food seriously—and have been doing so for generations—is manifest in the eighteenth-century painting opposite. Though the assembled aristocrats still retain their napkins, all other vestiges of etiquette have been abandoned in the pursuit of oysters.

satisfactory as equating a handshake with a relationship. To designate one who appreciates his food the French have such subtly calibrated terms as *gourmand*, *gourmet*, *bec fin*, and *fine fourchette*. We have only trencherman, which has more to do with appetite than appreciation and which, in any case, is of French derivation.

Where food is concerned, French curiosity and inventiveness are inexhaustible. The Frenchman will not only eat anything that looks remotely edible but will bring the full weight of culinary theory and logic to bear on it. If he mourns the loss of the pterodactyl it's because he's missed the chance to try it in a fricassee. Is the stegosaurus extinct? *Tant pis*! It might have made an interesting *roulade*. A decade and a half ago, when the largest mussel ever seen thereabouts—eighteen inches long if memory serves—was found near the mouth of the Rhône, a regional newspaper concluded its coverage of the event not with the announcement of its donation to a museum but with the words "It was delicious."

The French have created the Western world's most voluminous body of literature on the subject of gastronomy—indeed, the only one worth the name—and the most highly standardized cuisine on earth. As an Italian observer quoted by Waverley Root remarked, "French cooking is formalized, technical, and scientific. Order Béarnaise sauce in 200 different French restaurants and you will get exactly the same sauce 200 times. Ask for Bolognese sauce in 200 different Italian restaurants and you will get 200 different versions of *ragù*." Moreover, it's a cuisine of mind-boggling exhaustiveness. The French restaurateur rash enough to adopt the American custom of offering "eggs any style," for example, might be asked to prepare any of the more than 350 egg dishes listed in *Larousse Gastronomique*.

To glance at a few more statistics culled from *Larousse*, the French repertory includes: 261 sauces; 95 sole preparations; 234 dishes in which chicken appears as the salient ingredient; 67 different soufflés; 106 ways of serving potatoes, not including their use in soups, stews, and the like; 306 soups; 133 veal dishes (plus 149 recipes for the glorification of the calf's inner organs); 47 artichoke specialties; 54 compound butters; 23 dishes in which truffles play the leading role; 30 ways of serving oysters; 21, 40, 42, and 43 ways of cooking pigeon, pheasant, quail, and partridge respectively; 50 eel dishes; and 52 salads. *Larousse* also lists 165 cheeses, of which the overwhelming majority are domestically produced; a figure some authorities would find unduly conservative, as they might any of the foregoing.

To quantify French cuisine, though, or define its component dishes is in no way to convey any idea of what it's all about. To say, for instance, that *tripes à la mode de Caen* is one of some fifteen widely recognized French dishes made from the stomachs of cattle and is cooked slowly in a sealed pot containing an ox's hoof, carrots, and onions, would be about as effective as defining Brigitte Bardot as one of 50 million featherless bipeds native to a country that occupies 212,000 square miles of Western Europe and that used to be called Gaul. Properly prepared and presented, tripe provides one of the most magnificently orchestrated experiences human genius has devised, and one as

fulfilling to its partisans as a Beethoven symphony or a late Rembrandt self-portrait are to theirs.

For the common man at least, the procurement of food had been a serious matter in France throughout the Middle Ages, when famine periodically reached pandemic levels and cannibalism was rife in the heartland—where, according to the eleventh-century monk Raoul Glaber, to stop for the night at a wayside inn was to risk appearing as the next afternoon's *plat du jour*. The situation had eased considerably by the late thirteenth century, however, and by the late fourteenth Frenchmen began to take a more serious interest in the quality, variety, and preparation of their meals.

It is from that period that *Le Viandier*, one of the first French cookbooks, compiled by Guillaume Tirel (or Tisel), dates. Tirel, known to gastronomic history as Taillevent, appears to have begun his illustrious career as a scullion in the royal kitchens sometime before 1326, when he was mentioned for the first time in an account of the coronation of Jeanne d'Evreaux, the bride of Charles the Fair. Apparently a precocious lad, Tirel became head cook to the Valois king Philippe VI, a position he held from 1346 to 1350, and was eventually appointed *chef de cuisine* and master of the garrisons of France by Charles V. At one point he was provided by Philippe with a house "in consideration of the good and pleasant services" he had rendered that monarch and for "those he hopes still to receive."

An idea of just how good and pleasant those services may have been is conveyed by Tirel's menu for a banquet served to the king toward the end of the century. Desserts aside, dinner on that occasion comprised fourteen dishes (served in three courses), of which three were made up of capons in various guises (with cinnamon broth, in spiced pies, and in sour grape juice), four were of other fowl, and two were of venison. New cabbage was the only vegetable, buttered bread and meat jellies were counted as dishes, and the festivities also included young hares stewed in vinegar and "a fine roast" of unspecified origin. In short, a meal as monotonously repetitive as most big medieval feeds but perhaps enlivened somewhat by Tirel's command of twenty-odd sauces, including "*saulce Robert*," his reading of the English roebuck sauce, of which a more refined version is still a mainstay of the French repertory and an excellent accompaniment to grilled meats.

Considered individually, some of Tirel's dishes still sound appetizing enough. They are not *haute cuisine* by a long shot, at least according to modern criteria, but part of the wholesome bourgeois tradition that is both the basis for and real glory of all French gastronomy. He cooked his chickens with good garden herbs, and there are worse recipes in use today than the one he recorded for hare, which he first spit-roasted, then cut up and cooked with diced pork fat and croutons in beef broth and wine. Such hashes as a *galimafrée* of chopped leg of mutton (flavored with ginger and stewed with minced onions in butter and vinegar), or a *morterel* (the dish known to Chaucer's Cook, who could "maken mortrewes and well bake a pie") of egg-bound pheasant, kid's leg, and tripe sound a lot tastier and more wholesome than several basically similar dishes that, swollen with hamburger "extender," are advertised

Le Viandier, *one of the first French cookbooks, was written in 1375 by Guillaume Tirel,* chef de cuisine *to Charles V. In addition to being a compendium of recipes, it gives a detailed picture of the tastes and manners of the medieval court. The cookbook brought its author recognition not only in his own lifetime but also in succeeding centuries. Indeed,* Le Viandier *was one of the first books printed in movable type, and the illustration opposite is from an early printed edition of the work. Fittingly, when Tirel died, a shield with three caldrons was emblazoned on his tombstone.*

on television today. Although a bit overspiced, one late-fourteenth-century recipe for a brewet of eels isn't essentially different from the *matelotes* still enjoyed around Bordeaux. Tirel's great weaknesses, and the weaknesses of medieval cooking in general, were a lack of true sauces—his were little more than soups thickened with bread—an ignorance of pacing, balance, and contrast, limited means of varying savors, aromas, textures, and colors, and a marked tendency to mistake quantity for quality and to pile one dish, however redundant or inappropriate, on another.

At about the same time Richard II, who was born in English-ruled Gascony, "was accounted the best and royallest viander of all Christian kings" and set the most magnificent table in Europe, entertaining as many as ten thousand guests at a sitting, supplying his hundreds of cooks with twenty-eight oxen and three hundred sheep each day and creating a vogue for frenchified recipes.

Charles VII, who in the next century succeeded in divesting the English of most of their French holdings, also set a fine table, thanks in large part to his mistress Agnès Sorel, who knew the way to a man's heart and wasn't above donning an apron to produce such delicacies as *salmis* of woodcock and *petites timbales* of truffled chicken forcemeat for the king's delectation. In the main, however, French gastronomy continued to concern itself more with gluttony than refinement. François I might employ Italian cooks—then universally acknowledged to be the best in the world—and dote on pale veal, fried calves' brains, and grilled calves' livers, but his feasts remained medieval at bottom. Nor were the court and clergy alone addicted to high living; the emergent bourgeoisie stuffed themselves four and five times daily, devouring quantities of meat that appalled discriminating Italian travelers—who also disapproved of the take-out fare that became the rage of Paris in the first half of the sixteenth century. "Rotisseurs, pastry cooks, will get you up a dinner for ten, twenty or thirty persons in less than an hour," the Venetian ambassador observed sourly, adding that the cost of some ready-made meals could have been justified only by the service of manna and roast phoenix and noting that his hosts were doing as much violence to their insides "as the Germans and Poles do by drinking too much."

If Italian cooks were popular in France before the advent of Catherine de Mèdicis, most of their potential contributions remained as esoteric as the fork. By and large the French continued to gorge on spit-roasted meats and the slow-cooked messes that issued from their cauldrons, with their imported *maîtres queux* adding little but the cachet of their presence to the cuisine. François I popularized garlic (which he ate crushed in butter as a restorative of strength and health), but neither he nor his subjects had much use for vegetables in general. Soups —products, of course, of the cauldron—remained immensely popular, so much so that several might be consumed at a sitting. With Catherine's arrival, however, all that began to change, although neither as abruptly nor as widely as might be supposed. Despite a variety of innovations, French gastronomy remained much as it had been for another full century and more.

It was during the reign of Henri III (below) that the Italian culinary practices introduced into France by his mother, Catherine de Mèdicis, reached their apogee; aperitifs were sipped at court, Italian chefs and pastrycooks were held in the highest esteem, and Henri himself affected an Italianate, two-pronged fork. But by and large, French gastronomy continued to concern itself more with gluttony than refinement. Though Henri might employ Italian chefs, his banquets remained, at bottom, the medieval feasts favored by his predecessors. One such forebear, Charles VIII, staged a banquet (right) that lasted for ten days and included more than two thousand guests.

The emergence of *la cuisine Française* as the crowning glory of Western gastronomy began during the reign of Henri IV of Navarre, the first of the Bourbon monarchs, a leader who restored stability and prosperity to France after years of warfare and privation and a man who preempted Herbert Hoover's best line by informing his subjects that he wished nothing less for them than a hen in every pot. Henri's circle of intimates included one François Pierre de La Varenne, who had begun his career as a lowly scullion in the kitchen of the king's sister, the duchesse de Bar, but later became a paragon among chefs. He also became an unofficial minister of state and Henri's go-between in affairs of the heart, moving the duchess to observe that he had "done better by carrying my brother's *poulets* [literally "chickens" but slang for "love letters"] than by larding mine."

La Varenne waged a one-man revolution in French cookery. The first great *saucier*, he abandoned the traditional practice of using highly spiced, bread-thickened broths as moistening agents for meats, substituting for them savory reductions of natural cooking juices, which he bound with the cooked flour-and-butter mixture now known as *roux*. To dress fish he hit on the ingenious notion of simmering their heads and trimmings with vegetables and aromatics to produce a *fumet*, or stock, that could be thickened with the same *roux* and subtly inflected with the bouquet of herbs, mushrooms, and truffles. He also brought a significant measure of logic and order to his menus, simplified them considerably, and did away with the heaping pyramids of ill-assorted meats favored by his predecessors.

Despite La Varenne's innovations and the relative refinement of the duchess's table, the king himself continued to eat much as he loved and gambled: ostentatiously and indiscriminately. His last predecessor, Henri III, the third son of Catherine de Mèdicis and a teenage brawler who transformed himself into a jackanapes of staggering preciosity during a sojourn in Venice, had dined as ambivalently as he had lived. Generally he would breakfast in bed on French soups and Italian sugar cakes and dine alone or in the company of a few intellectuals, daintily wielding a two-pronged fork while soft music was played in the background and consuming oysters, whale's tongue with orange sauce, and Italianate desserts. On occasion, however, all his restraint was thrown to the winds. Then, His transvestite Majesty would dye his hair violet, dress himself and his minions in bejewelled drag, requisition the half-naked ladies of his aging mother's Flying Squadron as waitresses, and stage *fêtes champêtres* of a decadence worthy of a film by Fellini. During his ill-fated reign the Italian culinary practices introduced by his mother reached their apogee as *apéritifs* were sipped for the first time at court and Italian chefs and pastry cooks were treated with a deference that soon rubbed off on their French counterparts and led to the formation of cooks' and bakers' guilds.

Except for a predilection for cream bonbons, Henri VI harbored none of his predecessor's elegant pretensions, effeminate tendencies, or gastronomic proclivities, and had no desire to dine—or do anything else for that matter—quietly and in privacy. He flaunted his appetites and excesses, performing life's most intimate functions before an audience, maintaining a noisy seraglio-cum-nursery that impelled one Italian envoy to remark that he had "never seen anything more like a brothel than this court" and sitting down to meals that conformed more closely to medieval than modern notions of gastronomy and more often than not degenerated into orgies.

In theory Henri's dinner menus embodied notions of orchestration and progression then being advanced by La Varenne, but dishes arrived helter-skelter, piled up in the traditional medieval manner, and often were forgotten as revelers tried to drink one another under the table or pretended to admire gilded set pieces that took the same worn-out forms dinner after dinner, year after year. Wines from Beaune, Pauillac, Anjou, Graves, Orléans, the Medoc, and elsewhere were guzzled immoderately, but the vineyards had been sadly neglected during the Wars of Religion and some idea of their quality—or at least the degree of connoisseurship attained by the guzzlers—may be had from the practice, then new, of drinking toasts. This took the form of passing a goblet from mouth to mouth until it reached the lips of the guest of honor, who was expected to eat the sodden gobbet of grilled bread at its bottom. Such was Henri's table, which is remembered today chiefly for its popularization of the napkin (tied around the neck to protect the ornate ruffs then worn) and for the ubiquitous cabbage dishes (cabbage with crows was a favorite of the time) that invested a lowly vegetable with regal status.

The publication of François Pierre de La Varenne's Le Cuisinier Français in 1651 was to profoundly influence French gastronomy, for it was La Varenne who perfected the superb sauces that are so integral to classical French cooking. The master chef frowned on the more traditional, heavily spiced, bread-thickened broths that accompanied meats (recipe above), preferring instead savory reductions of natural cooking juices, which he bound with flour and butter. La Varenne taught later generations of French chefs to forego excessive use of spices and to stress instead the inherent character of the ingredients used. Freshness became a virtue—and as such was demanded from the wandering vendors who sold Parisians most of their food (and who are fancifully depicted opposite in costumes appropriate to their specialized talents).

If the theories of La Varenne made little dent on the court gastronomy of his time, his books, *Le Cuisinier Français* in particular, were to have tremendous impact on succeeding generations. So, too, were those of Olivier de Serres, a visionary agriculturalist who operated a model farm during the reign of Henri IV, grew vegetables of a quality never before seen in France, and was encouraged by the king to preach the gospel of truck gardening to his subjects. Serres, whose metaphor "Ploughing and grazing are the two breasts of France" captured the imagination of compatriots always ready to consider larger issues in terms of the female anatomy, spurred a back-to-the-land movement, unavailingly extolled the virtues of the potato (then prized chiefly for its blossoms, which were worn as boutonnieres by the Germans as they later would be by Louis XVI), and was generally responsible for elevating vegetables to a position of high esteem in French cooking.

Between them, La Varenne and Serres put a virtual end to the heavily spiced cookery that remained in favor until around the end of Henri IV's reign; La Varenne, it would seem, through an underlying culinary integrity that impelled him to stress the inherent character of his ingredients and Serres because there was simply no need to spice vegetables whose chief virtues were their delicate flavor and relative freshness. Whether their efforts would have been so successful had

Habit de Cuisinier.

A Paris, Chez N. de Larmessin, Rüe S. Jacques à la Pome d'or.   Avec Privil. du R.

Habit de Paticier

Paris, Chez N. de Larmessin, Rüe S. Jacques à la Pome d'or.   Avec Privil. du Roy.

improvements in international trade not driven the cost of spices down to the point where their use no longer impressed anyone is debatable. Whatever the reasons, Frenchmen had at long last begun to find out how their foods really tasted and to enjoy them for what they were.

Cookery was slowly but surely beginning to achieve the status of a serious art and for perhaps the first time the nobility—and even royalty —wasn't above some participation, however dilettantish, in its development. Henri's prime minister, Philippe de Mornay, for example, is credited by some authorities with the invention of the white sauce that bears his name. The princesse de Conti, a lady-in-waiting to Marie de Mèdicis and the object, however briefly, of the affections of Marie's husband, Henri IV, is supposed to have wooed her royal lover with a rib of mutton dish that still bears her name (although the recipe may have been ghostwritten by Saupiquet, a master chef in the employ of the baron de la Vieuville and the great exponent of puff pastry). Whether these ladies ever actually toiled over a hot stove is conjectural,

Small markets, like the seventeenth-century one above, were the precursors of Les Halles, "the belly of Paris" and central market that was established in the nineteenth century. Here bread and poultry are sold on the Quai de Grands Augustins. At left is the Pont Neuf; in the background, the Louvre.

but the mere idea that they might have is in itself indicative of the heights of respectability to which cookery had risen.

Even the king himself was reputed to have tried his hand at an occasional ragout, but whether he did or not, it's certain that Henri's successor, Louis XIII, was an enthusiastic if not overly accomplished amateur cook who specialized in jams, game, and in eggs, which he prepared "a hundred different ways." Unfortunately, neither his conserves nor his game and egg dishes seem to have been very original and neither he nor his reign added anything of significance to the repertory. If he failed to produce a dish fit for any king but himself, however, he at least made it clear that the culinary art—and not merely its end products—was worthy of regal investigation.

French gastronomy really came into its own during the reign of Louis XIV. The Sun King was an indiscriminate glutton who at the top of his form was capable of putting away four soups, a pheasant, a partridge, a joint of mutton, a couple of slabs of ham, a plateful of cakes, and a half-dozen or so eggs at a sitting, along with an assortment of fruits and jams. (Impressive as such an intake may sound, it would hardly have whetted the appetite of the fabled American, Diamond Jim Brady, who at a typical dinner—his fifth and penultimate meal of the day—would ingest three dozen of the largest Lynnhaven oysters available before destroying six crabs, washing them down with at least a couple of bowls of green turtle soup and then getting down to serious business: a half-dozen lobsters, a brace of canvasback ducks, two copious helpings of diamondback turtle, a thick sirloin steak, a platter of pastries, and a two-pound box of chocolates, all—with the possible exception of the chocolates—appropriately garnished with vegetables. It should be noted, though, that comparing the two men is a bit like pitting a smelt against a great white shark; at his death it was discovered that Louis's intestine was only twice normal length and that he was feeding a tapeworm besides, while an autopsy performed on Brady revealed a stomach with six times average capacity.)

Louis justified his exaggerated gourmandism with the glib explanation: "One works well who dines well." And while he, like many of his predecessors, tended to confuse tonnage with quality, the foods he consumed so avidly were prepared and served with more style than any of his forebears had encountered. La Varenne's great book, which was to become holy scripture to partisans of the so-called new cuisine, was published in 1651, the eighth year of Louis's reign, and forty years later, a quarter-century before that reign ended, Massialot's significantly titled *Le Cuisinier Royal et Bourgeois*, another landmark work, demonstrated the extent to which the application of La Varenne's theories had reshaped and varied French cookery.

Massialot's book makes clear that heavy, spiced dishes smeared with almond pastes had given way to meats served simply in their own juices, that fresh vegetables were braised in savory stocks, and that *duxelles* of subtly scented mushroom forcemeat invested all manner of dishes with unprecedented elegance. It also demonstrates that dishes were meant to be savored individually, in a logical progression worked out as intricately as a musical composition. Applying La Varenne's

91

principles, one culinary genius added chicken or veal stock and cream to the master's basic *roux* to create a superb sauce that immediately became a mainstay of French—and later international—cookery: sauce Béchamel, which he named for Louis's lord steward, thereby depriving his own name of its rightful place in history. Clear consommés and light *potages* replaced many of the thick, ill-defined soups that had simmered in catch-all cauldrons since the early Middle Ages. One such, *consommé a la Colbert*, named for one of the king's finance ministers, was a gleaming chicken soup garnished with shredded vegetables and poached eggs. A great many of the dishes created during Louis's long reign were named for court personages, sometimes no doubt out of sheer sycophancy but more often than one might suspect because of a courtier's manifest interest or direct intervention in their creation.

All this interest in gastronomy precipitated fierce rivalries, with courtiers vying for the distinction of setting the most resplendent table or staging the most magnificent banquet. Indeed, it was one such blow-out that led directly to the downfall of Colbert's predecessor, Nicolas Fouquet, and indirectly to the construction of Versailles.

When Louis XIV acceded to the throne in 1643, courtiers still spat on the floors of the Louvre and urinated on its staircases. Still, the palace, as well as the royal residence at Fontainebleau, was opulent enough in its sprawling, planless fashion and presumably adequate to the needs and self-esteem of a monarch who was then five years old. And so they still seemed eighteen years later, when the king, now quit of the regent, alighted one hot summer afternoon in the driveway of his chief minister, the aforementioned Fouquet. The occasion was a housewarming, for work had just been finished on a little hideaway built largely with funds the host had, as finance minister, abstracted from the royal till.

Designed by the architect Le Vau, set in magnificent gardens planned by Lenôtre, and decorated by the painter Le Brun, Vaux-le-Vicomte was a splendiferous white edifice the like of which had never before been seen. In keeping with its grandeur the evening's entertainment was to be provided by the composer Lully and a promising young playwright named Molière. Dinner would be supervised by none other than Vatel, the renowned *maître d'hotel*, who had stocked the kitchens with the finest bottles Beaune and Champagne had to offer. The evening was to conclude with a crescendo of fireworks of which the very heavens, according to a poet on hand for the festivities, would grow jealous. The fireworks took place somewhat earlier than scheduled.

His Majesty, duly impressed with the appurtenances and amenities of Fouquet's modest digs, eventually was steered toward Vatel's domain, where the table had been set with what Louis described with seeming ingenuousness as "admirable plate." "*Ah, oui,*" one can almost hear him murmuring as Fouquet took the bait, begged pardon and explained, ahem, that the service was not plate, but gold. Springing the trap, Louis retorted: "We have nothing like this at the Louvre." Three weeks later Fouquet was in the slammer, his property confiscated, and the king had begun arrangements for an even more spectacular pleasure dome of his own—Versailles.

It was during the reign of Louis XIV that French gastronomy came into its own. The Sun King's reign was a time of gastronomic excitation and culinary inventiveness—but none of the gifted chefs in Louis's employ were equipped to deal with the problems posed by state banquets. The limitations of palace and protocol were simply overwhelming. The distance between the kitchens and the halls of state was usually considerable; food had to be carried down long, drafty corridors and then past the ranks of courtiers, tasters, and other functionaries. The end result, as can be seen opposite, was that dishes arrived helter-skelter and lukewarm.

LE DINE DV ROY A L'HOTEL DE VILLE DE PARIS

Versailles housed upward of a thousand ranking tenants while Louis was in residence there. Legend has it that the king expected them all to excel in the kitchen and that the surest way to curry his favor was to invent a dish that pleased him. If so, life must have been hell on earth for the hundreds of professionals in residence, with the marquis de so-and-so, the duc de such-and-such, the royal mistress-of-the-moment, or any halfway well-connected fool mincing into the king's kitchens, making unholy messes of the *batterie de cuisine*, throwing off everyone's timing, coercing chefs into producing misconceived inspirations in quantity, and making general nuisances of themselves any time they had a creative seizure.

However unwelcome they may have been in his kitchens, several members of Louis's entourage made notable contributions to French gastronomy. His queen, Maria Theresa, may have bored him in bed but

94

she enlivened his table with chocolate, omelets, various sauces (including the still-invaluable *sauce Espagnole*), the *bizcochos* the French were to call *bisquits*, and a sumptuous soup called *olla podrida*—all brought from her native Spain. One of his innumerable mistresses, Mme de Montespan, tempted him with, among other things, an original lark pâté and at least one sauce of her own devising. Another inamorata, Mme de Maintenon, may or may not have invented the vegetable-and-ham garnish and several dishes that still bear her name, but she was to have a profound and continuing effect on French gastronomy by founding an academy for girls that eventually became the Cordon Bleu school of cooking. The *petit four*, too, that most exquisite of pastries, was created expressly for Louis's delectation and (or so the story goes) won a place at court for the country aristocrat who had the "rare courage, artistry and taste" to serve his royal visitor with a single tiny cake on an immense platter. Finally, the marquis de Louvois, Louis's war minister, is generally credited with the invention of the chocolate, coffee, and whipped cream drink named for him.

The bulk of these accounts, and many others like them, may well be apocryphal; no one knows how many recipes, fobbed off as their own by ambitious courtiers, were actually the work of handsomely bribed professionals. Nevertheless, the Grand Monarch's reign was a time of both gastronomic excitation and culinary imaginativeness, a time when French cuisine, as it was to be known thenceforth, was forged.

That excitation was by no means restricted to Versailles and the upper crust, but swept across France and captured the imagination of the common man. La Varenne's *Le Cuisinier Français* went through eight printings in seventy-five years. A cookbook by Nicolas de Bonnefons ran through five editions in about the same length of time and others, many of them combining recipes with standards of etiquette set at court, did almost as well. *Petits pois*, the *piselli novelli* introduced a century and more earlier by Catherine de Mèdicis, took first Versailles and then the nation by storm. The king was reputed to ingest no fewer than a hundred oysters at a sitting, ergo the bourgeoisie had to gorge on as many as their purses would allow, downing them raw or, if that began to cloy, grilling them, buttered and peppered, on the half shell. *Pot-à-oie*, an ostentatious preparation in which a large goose was stuffed with successively smaller birds, was all the rage, and if a host could afford to serve only the stuffing, leaving the goose for the servants, so much the better for his *amour propre*.

The stiff, formal banquet at left took place on the Giudecca in Venice in 1755. Among the more illustrious surnames listed beneath the illustration are Tiepolo, Polo, Foscari, Loredan, and Pisani. Significantly, forks are very much in evidence, the use of this eating implement having been established throughout most of Europe by this time.

Etiquette and protocol were twin manias at Versailles but didn't altogether conform with modern notions of the social niceties. The Sun King had no use for the fork and less for its users. Punctilious to the point of unfailingly raising his hat to charwomen, he ate with his fingers throughout his life and expected his guests to do the same. Indeed, the fork was held in such low esteem at court that one imposter, posing as a marquis on a free-loading tour of the provinces, gave himself away by impaling an olive with one while dining with the military commandant of Bayonne. Small talk—or any conversation—was as unwelcome as the fork at the king's table, possibly because Louis's mouth was full from the moment he sat down until he hoisted his bulk

A dinner for the King, Jan.ʸ 7.ᵗʰ

A Twenty five Dish Table.

Promising though English cuisine seemed for a time, the influence of Cromwell and Puritanism was to prevent it from achieving its full potential. One could hardly fault the available culinary resources, yet this budding cuisine nonetheless evolved into a monotonous round of plain meats and boiled vegetables. The dinner at left, served to King George II, contained twenty-five dishes—only one of which was meatless.

out of his chair at meal's end. Whatever the reason, those silent dinners *au grand couvert* (that is to say, in the presence of the full court) must have been trying indeed for a screech of popinjays to whom gossip and backchat were far less dispensable than bread. Even more curious was the occasional dinner *au public*, when any more or less presentable citizen of the realm was privileged to line up and derive whatever edification he might from a glimpse of the monarch feeding his face.

Curiously, Louis's contempt for the fork wasn't shared by all his subjects, and the implement was in common use in Paris by the mid-seventeenth century. Nor did the well-to-do Parisian restrict himself to two meals a day, as his king did (the royal breakfast, white bread and watered wine, hardly conformed to Louis's definition of a meal and his serious eating took place at about one o'clock in the afternoon and again late in the evening). Instead, he ate breakfast, a hearty lunch, a *gousté* comparable to the English high tea, and an eight o'clock supper. Bread had by then become a household staple, with the bourgeoisie consuming a pound a day per capita and country folk twice as much, although it was deemed infra dig at court.

Sardines, oddly, were thought to enhance the flavor of wine, which for the most part was drunk in the year of its vintage. Champagne, originally a red still wine, had by the waning years of the century—and largely through the intervention of a Benedictine monk, Dom Pierre Pérignon—been transformed into something much like the bubbly bottled under his name today. But champagne didn't come into widespread use until well into the 1770's because the glassblower's art was incapable of devising a bottle that could withstand the pressure of fermentation. Cider played a role of some importance in the northwest, where apples grew better than grapes, but, as the modern social historian W. H. Lewis remarks, it "was thought by right-minded men to be God's judgment on the Normans for their rascality."

The Parisian of means took his food seriously during Louis's reign, modeled the management of his household on that of the king and its appearance on that of the Hotel de Rambouillet, built by the Italian-born marquise de Rambouillet, whose glittering salon was her answer to what she considered the loutishness of life at court. His dining room —itself a recent innovation—was papered, usually in pale blue, and the centerpiece of his table was an elaborately wrought *surtout* containing salt, pepper, spices, and the toothpicks whose use was by then considered a bit more genteel than gouging at one's molars with the point of a knife. His guests no longer brought their own implements but found their places set with a knife (black-handled during Lent, white the rest of the year), fork, and spoon. Toward the end of the reign soup was no longer drunk from a two-handled communal bowl but ladled into individual bowls by the diners, who by then were expected to have the good grace not to put spoons in their mouths before dipping them into the tureen. The trencher had long since given way to porcelain dishware, and what little spitting occurred was accomplished discreetly, with the head averted. Theatrical set pieces, the subtleties that for so long could be counted on to produce exclamations of feigned astonishment, were a thing of the past. Indeed, it was by then bad form to discuss any aspect of the meal itself.

Just what the composition of that meal may have been remains somewhat speculative, since most surviving descriptions have to do with dinners served in grander surroundings. The menu can't have been much different in principle from those of our host's betters, though, for the few cookbooks ostensibly written for his use, such as Massialot's, drew no meaningful social distinctions insofar as the food itself was concerned. In all probability a good town supper (as the evening meal was then called) would begin with some such *entrée* as calf's head *vinaigrette*, prepared and served much as it is in restaurants today, or beef tongue (soup, according to a late seventeenth-century book written for the instruction of schoolchildren, was for "ordinary hunger" and not the stuff of a "festive" meal).

The *entrée* might be followed by a "*potage*" of venison stewed with turnips or partridges with cabbage. Depending on the host's means, his guests might then get down to such matters of substance as the *pot-à-oie* mentioned earlier, along with any or all of such offerings as roast kid with sorrel sauce, perhaps a galantine of chicken (almost certainly chicken in some form), suckling pig, rabbit *à l'orange*, filet of beef with cucumbers, and roast quarter of veal. Melon usually preceded the roast (or roasts), oranges were served with meat, and hors d'oeuvres, which weren't then what they are today, accompanied each service, generally taking the form of a simple but by no means insubstantial dish. A menu of 1662, for example, includes such throwaway items as two salads, fried sheeps' testicles, sliced roast beef with kidneys, and chickens roasted in embers. Moreover, cold salmon, ham, or beef tongue (if it hadn't appeared as an *entrée*) were customarily arranged around the *surtout*, presumably for the relief of guests who weren't up to making conversation between services. The festivities would conclude with cakes, assorted jellies, pastries, almonds and rosewater, and possibly an after-dinner liqueur, but no coffee. Wine, of course, was served throughout.

If the French had taken the gastronomic lead, the English adopted a somewhat ambivalent attitude toward culinary advances across the Channel. On the one hand they loudly proclaimed the sovereignty of bluff English cooking and, on the other, sent their own cooks to France for instruction. The English had come a long way from the heavy, basically Oriental, sugar-and-spice cuisine on which Henry VIII had fattened himself, and from the quaint notions of gastronomy prevalent in the early Elizabethan period, when one Andrewe Boorde, a self-

By the seventeenth century, the hearty, robust fare of the Low Countries was being augmented by exotic fruits brought home in vessels owned by the Dutch East India Company. Indeed, painter Jan Davidsz. de Heem made his home in Antwerp because there he could find the best of the rare fruits that crowd such still lifes as the one below. At right, Pieter Bruegel's Peasant Wedding.

styled dietician, informed his countrymen that "Pygges, specially some pygges, is nutrytve, so be it the pygg be fleed, the skin taken off and then stewed with restoratives, as a cocke is stewed to make a gelye."

Cookbooks were far more numerous in seventeenth-century England than in France, the enormous success of La Varenne's and Bonnefons's works notwithstanding, and free-lance cooks, or freecooks, hired by the day as they were in Roman times, often did quite well for themselves. Pepys writes of hiring one of these, who prepared a "pretty dinner" of a brace of stewed carp, a jowl of salmon, six roast chickens, neats' tongues, a tansy, and cheese, leaving his temporary employer free to make "Merry all the afternoon, talking, singing, and piping on the flageolet."

Promising as the English cuisine seemed for a time, cookery in England was never really to recover from the plainness inflicted on it by Cromwell and Puritanism. Perhaps to say it was never to recover is to take an outsider's biased view of the matter; "I have discovered to my stupefaction," Waverley Root has written, "that the English cook that way because that is the way they like it." Like it or not, they made of a budding cuisine, with a wealth of culinary resources to draw upon, the monotonous round of plain meats and boiled vegetables that long ago became a standing joke throughout the non-English world.

Pepys may have found his English food enjoyable (at least when he didn't entrust it to his wife's erratic cooking), Charles II might be impressed enough with his roast beef to dub it "Sir Loin" in a mock knighting, and Patrick Lamb, the master cook at St. James's Palace, might boast of banquets that were the envy of all Europe, but contemporaneous sojourners from France found little to admire at the English table. One, named Misson, noted that those noblemen who employed

French cooks ate decently in the French style but that the "middling sort of people" subjected themselves to a dreary diet of unlarded roasts and boiled salt meats, varying it only with "five or six heaps of cabbage, carrots, turnips and some other herbs or roots" and with their omnipresent puddings served "fifty several ways." But unappetizing as it all may sound, the English did like their cooking that way, or so at least it would seem from the typical account of one English traveler in Italy who complained of finding "raw ham, Bologna sausages, figs and melons" there, but "no boiled leg of pork and pease pudding. No bubble-and-squeak."

Elsewhere in northern Europe, French taste, French manners, and French gastronomy prevailed at court and in the noble houses, while the bourgeoisie, in large part newly prosperous, developed solid, robust cuisines much like those they enjoy today, washing down foods rich in fats and carbohydrates with prodigious quantities of beer and hard liquor and scandalizing their temperate neighbors to the south.

In the Low Countries the people cultivated a taste for the exotic fruits brought home by ships of the Dutch East India Company and in the process gave rise to a whole new school of still-life painting epito-

The eighteenth-century German chef (right), like the rest of the German population, saw little of beef. Pork, however, was ubiquitous, and the hog-slaughtering scene depicted below could have taken place anywhere in the country. The finest pigs were raised in Westphalia, and every locality boasted its own variety of sausage. The staples of pork and sausage were occasionally augmented with freshly caught fish (below, right), but only at the tables of the well-to-do.

mized by Jan Davidsz. de Heem, who chose to live and work in Antwerp simply because "there one could have rare fruits of all kinds . . . to draw from life." The Dutch and Flemish ate the fatty stews they called *Hutsepot* and *hotchepot* respectively, beer-braised beef *carbonnades*, the fish-and-wine soup known as *waterzoï*, herrings and fat cheeses, salt cod and shellfish, pancakes and waffles. They grew the finest vegetables in northern Europe in the seventeenth century, including the Belgian endive, and the Dutch produced exceptionally good butter, cookies, and chocolates. They also distilled very good gin, knocked it back with an awesome prodigality, and exported what was left to England, where it was to provide another artist, Hogarth, with the sort of opportunity Eastern fruit afforded de Heem. The East India Company was also responsible for the introduction of *rijsttafel*, a kind of Indonesian smorgasbord that took Holland by storm.

The Scandinavians, who had combined their Viking propensities with Latinate elegance during the Renaissance, took to the new French sauces with notable enthusiasm, freely adapting them to their own taste for excessive richness, and irrigating their systems with oceanic quantities of beer, *aquavit,* and sweetened wines (perhaps the cold climate

had something to do with their love of sweets; when the price of sugar ceased to be prohibitive around the mid-sixteenth century it was consumed in alarming proportions).

The smorgasbord, the cold table laden with an infinitely varied array of dishes, had originated perhaps as early as Viking times, when celebrants traveled considerable distances to banquet halls to proudly add their regional specialties to the groaning board. Fish, of course, had long been the stable protein of the Scandinavian diet, and such traditional preparations as the marinated fresh salmon known as *gravad lax* retained their Scandinavian identity. Nonetheless, such Gallic specialties as *mousse de brochet* were much in evidence.

Pork and smoked wurst, dark bread and beer, lentils and cabbage, soups with liver dumplings, an occasional rabbit or goose—these were the chief components of a burgher's meal in what is now Germany. Prussian court cuisine became thoroughly gallicized under Frederick the Great, but other highborn Teutons resisted the trend. Lisolette, for one, German wife of the duc d'Orléans, is supposed to have acquainted Parisians with the delights of pickled herring, blood sausage, and raw cured ham. But she disdained their attempts to reciprocate and pined for the pork-laden sauerkraut of her homeland, little suspecting that, as *choucroûte garni*, it would one day become a specialty of the local Parisian *brasserie*.

Sauerkraut, apparently imported from China by the Tartars much

Unlike the Dutch and Flemish, who grew the finest vegetables in northern Europe, the Germans raised hardly any green vegetables commercially until well into the nineteenth century. However, individual garden patches did augment a diet largely composed of rye, cabbage, root crops, and wheat. The harvest of the last is shown in both Germany (left) and Italy (above). German chefs (right) vitalized what would have been a hopelessly monotonous cuisine with a wide variety of soups, a mandatory course at almost every meal.

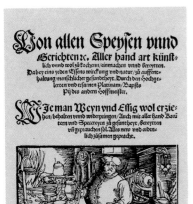

earlier, also loomed large in the cookery of the Magyars, who dressed it with sour cream (this too traceable to the Tartars) to produce *Szekelys gulyàs*, as it did in a variety of Slavic dishes, including the early peasant version of borscht. Later on, the meat *gulyàs*, or ragout, was of course liberally spiced with paprika, a tangy product of the American capsicum pepper brought to Budapest by the Ottoman Turks, who also brought *baclava* into the city, where it was filled with fruit and renamed *Strudel*. (In 1683 the Turks inadvertently were to play a decisive role in the invention of the *croissant*, when a Viennese baker noticed that his dough was quivering oddly, realized the vibration was caused by the distant boom of mines exploding against the city's outer walls, and alerted the defense forces. Rewarded with a post in the royal kitchen, he celebrated by shaping his rolls like the crescent moon of the Turkish flag. Later, Marie Antoinette brought the resultant *kipfel* to Paris, where the French, with their inimitable touch, enriched the dough and—*Voila*!—a national breakfast roll whose texture and flavor are determined by its shape.)

Poland had acquired its own preemptive version of Catherine de Mèdicis in 1518, when the princess Bona Sforza traveled to Cracow to marry the aging king Sigismund I and arrived with a battalion of cooks and gardeners in her wake. A great beauty and extremely popular at first, she wound up incurring the undying enmity of the population at large, but not before she had radically altered its eating habits by adding so many vegetables to the Polish diet that the word *wloszcyzna*, meaning "things Italian," had to be coined as a generic term for such innovations as the beet, cucumber, eggplant, and Savoy cabbage. Court gastronomy underwent another upheaval in 1573, when Catherine de Mèdicis's son Henri of Valois, through one of those Byzantine chains of circumstance that kept geneologists busy all over Europe, acceded to the Polish throne. Henri didn't stick around very long, skipping out in the dead of night when the good news reached Warwel Castle that his brother Charles was dead and the French throne was vacant. In his brief three years in Poland, however, he had shifted the emphasis from Italian to French cookery.

Only Russia remained relatively untouched by the eastward spread of French culinary influence, with much of its population subsisting on salt fish, black bread, cabbage, *kasha*, and sour cream, and eating quantities of the little raised pancakes called *blini* during the week before Lent. The frenchification of Russian gastronomy was to come much later and, when it did, was to produce a curious backlash that made dining *à la russe* the rage of Paris society by 1816.

For all its technical advances, French gastronomy during the reign of Louis XIV had been characterized by pomp, gluttony, and the futile, often ruinous attempts of the bourgeoisie to dine as regally as did their king. With Louis's long reign finally ended, dining in France took on more reasonable dimensions and pointed itself in a more fruitful direction. During the regency of Philippe d'Orléans, himself an amateur pastry maker, refinement, delicacy, and intimacy became the order of the day. Gone were the dinners *au grand couvert* or *au public*; in their stead the regent introduced the *petit souper*, an informal gathering of noblemen and their mistresses (or, in a pinch, their wives).

Taking his cue from the regent, Louis XV interested himself in food, learned to cook and, upon reaching his majority, continued the custom of the "little supper," giving it a twist or two his mentor hadn't foreseen. The presence of servants, it seems, cramped the royal style, especially when some particularly appetizing morsel appeared on the arm of one of his noble honchos. The first solution to this awkward state of affairs was to assemble the male guests in the kitchen and have them whip up lesser components of the meal while the king busied himself with the main "dish." Unfortunately, the scheme had a serious drawback for the male guests: an undisturbed dalliance with the ladies hardly could be realized while the gentlemen slaved over their stoves. After some high-level brainstorming a better one was devised whereby the dinner table sank from the room between courses, to be reset and replenished by servants on the floor below, while guests were "freed of all embarrassment and need not blush on being caught unawares." Precisely what reactions the unblushing Mme Du Barry and the other members of Louis's entourage may have had to the sudden materialization of a gaping chasm where the dinner table had been no contemporary bothered to record.

Once again French gourmets were agog over a new cuisine; a cuisine characterized by simplicity, ingenuity, harmony, and, above all,

The samovar is uniquely Russian. A charcoal-heated central column keeps water always at a boil; tea, steeping in a pot on top, is likewise kept hot. The steaming samovar was in itself a symbol of hospitality, and could be found at the center of any Russian gathering. It is, for example, the focal point of this convivial Moscow café scene.

lightness. As Louis Sebastien Mercier was to remark toward the end of the reign, "The dishes of the present day are very light, and they have a particular delicacy and perfume. . . . Who could enumerate all the dishes of the new Cuisine? It is an absolutely new idiom." (Mercier went on to mention viands "fashioned with such art that I could not imagine what they were"—a characteristic of *haute cuisine* that was to obtain until just the last few years, when a number of young Turks began to develop still another new cuisine, this one designed to emphasize, not mask, the basic nature of their materials.)

Light the individual dish may have been, but its very lightness was a calculated spur to gluttony. "The secret has been discovered," Mercier confided to readers of his *Tableau de Paris*, "of enabling us to eat more and to eat better, as also to digest more rapidly." Rapid digestion, he didn't trouble to add, facilitated an early return to the fray.

And once again the nobility betook itself to the kitchen, with, it would seem, half the members of court imploring chefs to create new dishes in their names and often tying on an apron themselves. While Voltaire complained that his compatriots' gluttony was numbing their mental faculties, Maria Leszczynska, the king's Polish wife (who, incidentally, popularized the lentil), was inspiring the royal chef to create *bouchées à la reine*, *poularde à la reine*, and *consommé à la reine* (all still in the repertory), the princesse de Soubise lent her name to a cutlet, the duchesse de Mailly gave hers to a leg of lamb, and the duc de Villeroi, marshal of France, was busy compounding a frying batter. The era's most spectacular *tour de force*, though, was pulled off by the duc de Richelieu, a grandnephew of the cardinal and a notable rake reputed to have staged nude *petits soupers*.

At one point during the Seven Years' War Richelieu magnanimously invited a gaggle of captured Hanoverian royalty to dinner, only to be informed by his chef that the field kitchen was stocked with nothing but a large carcass of beef and a few root vegetables. Undismayed, he sat down and composed what is probably the most extraordinary menu of all time: a six-course meal in which beef figured in every one of the twenty-two dishes, desserts included. So sure of its success was Richelieu, who seems to have known his food a lot better than his distraught chef did, that he informed that worthy and his *maître d'hotel* that, "If by any unhappy chance, this meal turns out to be not very good, I shall withhold from the wages of Maret and Roquelère a fine of 100 pistols. Go," he added, "and entertain no more doubts."

The meal unquestionably was a bit odd but, in view of the limited resources, incredibly varied and would have been unimaginable before the advent of the new cuisine. As *Larousse Gastronomique* sums it up, "This menu, strange as its composition may seem, is perfectly orthodox. Structurally, it obeys all the rules which were in force at this period concerning the organization of important meals."

In the mid-eighteenth century, when Jean Chardin painted the kitchen maid at left, cookery of any pretension still required a large staff. The closed-top range had not as yet been invented, and, consequently, a multiple-dish meal might require as many cooks as there were courses. Without the aid of labor-saving devices, life belowstairs was for the most part a constant round of menial, tedious tasks. The boredom on the young woman's face is obvious as she pauses momentarily from the drudgery of paring vegetables.

When a landmark cookbook, *The Gifts of Comus*, appeared in 1739, cookery of any pretension still required large kitchen staffs. Closed-top ranges and adjustable heat were still unknown and wouldn't appear until the early nineteenth century. Consequently a multiple-dish meal might require almost as many cooks as there were hot dishes. "I realize," wrote Marin, the author of the book in question, *maître d'hotel* of the prince de Soubise, and a leading exponent of the new cuisine, "that the cuisine of Comus is not practical for all, but with proper pots and pans, fresh food purchased each morning and a good bouillon, even third-class persons can dine with grace." That a culinary savant might deign to address the lower classes was startling enough in itself. Even more so was the fact that Marin was as willing to learn from as to educate them. His book was the first to make extensive use of recipes derived from lowly and provincial origins and, as such, was to have incalculable impact on the future of French gastronomy.

Marin's book contained recipes for no fewer than one hundred sauces and for such rarified dishes as the cock's comb and carp roe omelet he created for the king. On the other hand, it featured such robust regional fare as beef stew *à la Lyonnaise* and the anchovy-larded, garlicky veal cutlets of Provence. Nor did it disdain such inelegant *abats* as pigs' ears, tails, and snouts, the muzzles of oxen, or anything else the thrifty housewife might put to good use. Marin's chief rival, Menon, whose *Nouveau Traité de la Cuisine* appeared the same year, at first scorned the "low meats" he deemed fit only for the low-born. His dishes, he announced superciliously, used "only those parts and cuts that are known to the better classes." Menon came off his high horse when it became apparent that Marin had a runaway bestseller on his hands while the bourgeoisie were in no way receptive to his own hauteur, even when it was masked by a title like *La Cuisinière Bourgeoise*, which appeared in 1746. With his next book he reversed his previous prejudices altogether. It was titled *Suppers of the Court*, but it was filled with recipes for "low meats," and various villagers' ragouts and peasant stews.

Marin's and Menon's great contributions to French gastronomy lay in their lowering of the illogical barrier that tradition and physical isolation had erected between *haute cuisine* and bourgeois, even peasant, cookery and between the food of Paris and the provinces, their standardization of culinary practices, and the impetus they gave to good home cooking. On the foundations they laid the French were to build a cuisine capable of accommodating the most ethereal and the earthiest dishes at the same table; a cuisine that transcended such considerations as monetary means, social cachet, and the relative acceptability of raw materials so long as they were fresh, demanding only integrity, zeal, and a commitment to excellence. At their most desperate juncture Parisians may have been reduced to eating rat during the siege of 1870–71, but it's safe to say nobody before or since has eaten better prepared rat. As a celebrated chef of the period, Thomas Genin, noted with that unquenchable, analytic Gallic interest in all things ingestible, the rat "was repulsive to the touch but its flesh of tremendous quality: delicate but not too insipid. Well seasoned, it is perfect."

7

Masters of Their Art

The coal is killing us!
Antonin Carême

IT WAS YANKEE INGENUITY, curiously enough, that wrought the next great revolution in French—and, for that matter, world—gastronomy. The Yankee responsible was the Bavarian nobleman Count Rumford—and thereby hangs a tale.

For all their vaunted inventiveness in the kitchen, the French were artists, not mechanics, and had not by the late eighteenth century produced a really workable cooking device. Carême, perhaps the most celebrated chef of all time and architect (his term) of hundreds of dishes of stupefying complexity, complained bitterly of the cumbersome charcoal-burning *paillasses* within which he had to submit his delicately wrought fantasies to direct contact with live embers. Dishes were often scorched beyond redemption, sometimes caught fire, and always required individual attention, thereby compounding confusion by making inordinately large kitchen staffs prerequisite to cookery of any pretension whatever. Other "stoves," in reality nothing but warming ovens, had to be fired up repeatedly and then emptied of hot coals—a laborious and often frustrating operation and one that made it impossible to maintain even temperatures.

When the American Revolution broke out, one Benjamin Thompson, a Massachusetts Tory, hied himself to England, where he appears to have spent much of his self-imposed exile cogitating on the shortcomings of the kitchen equipment then in use. Whether his meditations were spurred by the quality of English food remains moot, but he eventually turned up in Bavaria, where in 1789 he installed the prototype of the modern kitchen range in a noble house, conducted further research, and was ennobled for scientific contributions that, among other things, made the cooking of sauerkraut a less chancy affair than it had been before his arrival on the scene. As Count Rumford, he settled in Munich and there, in those preinflationary days, managed to feed 1,200 poor at a cost of $3.44 per day for the lot, using a range that consumed a minimum of fuel. Ultimately he devised a true closed-topped range that derived maximum benefits from a relatively small fire by means of an ingenious system of flues and dampers.

Carême didn't live to avail himself of the fruits of Thompson's

Tour d'Argent was founded in Paris in 1582, though at that time the world-famous restaurant was a superior hostelry frequented by kings and other members of the aristocracy. In the painting opposite, Fréderic, who was the restaurant's proprietor at the turn of the century, carves the house specialty. Roast duckling remains one of the outstanding entrées in the Tour d' Argent repertoire.

labors, succumbing at forty-nine, possibly from the effects of overexposure to cooking fumes. As one eulogist remarked, he was "burnt out by the flame of his genius and the fuel of his ovens." During the course of his truncated career, however, he had established the ground rules for *la cuisine classique*, the style that dominated French gastronomy during and for some time after the Napoleonic era, providing the basis upon which much of France's reputation for culinary superiority still rests.

Carême was born in Paris in 1784, supposedly the descendant of a cook to Pope Leo X. Antonin (né Marie-Antoine) was sent forth into the world at an extremely tender age by a father who, bankrupted by his own fecundity (there were twenty-five siblings), blew his offspring to a good tavern dinner, informed him at some point between the hors d'oeuvres and dessert of the boundless opportunities that were his for the taking—and abandoned the lad. According to Prosper Montagné, author of *Larousse Gastronomique* and himself a great chef, "Destiny led him to a humble cookshop. . . . A precarious beginning!"

Whether it was destiny or the prospect of an occasional slice of ham or hunk of sausage that led Carême to his precarious beginning is debatable. In any case he is next heard of as a scullion in the kitchen of a restaurant where, to take a second helping of Montagné's rich prose, "His passionate application to work, his frenzy for learning, his wise intuition for the secrets and resources of his art, his progress from such a sudden and easy beginning, all these qualities designated him as a person of exceptional quality."

Carême seems indeed to have been a person of exceptional quality and soon was recognized as such by Bailly, a renowned *pâtissier* to the carriage trade who operated a shop on the rue Vivienne and numbered Talleyrand (of whom we'll hear more later) among his patrons. By the time he was seventeen, Carême was a rising star being given plenty of encouragement by Bailly, who knew a born pastrycook when he saw one. "This good master," his young protégé was to write later in life, "showed a lively interest in me. He allowed me to leave work in order to draw in the print room."

Scholars are heavily indebted to Bailly's kindliness and perspicacity; Carême's drawings are at least as instructive to gustatory historians as Villard de Honnecourt's are to students of medieval architecture or Andreas Vesalius's anatomical studies are to researchers in Renaissance medicine. His designs, based on a sedulous study of architectural prints, today seem almost parodies of Napoleonic pomp, but Bailly instantly recognized them as reflections of the neoclassical spirit that reigned just after Bonaparte's negotiation of the Peace of Amiens and allowed his assistant to translate them into *pièces montées* for presentation at the consul's state dinners. (Elaborate outgrowths of the "sotelties" of an earlier age, these *pièces montées* looked far too good to eat and in fact often were constructed of inedible materials.)

In any case, Napoleon was far more interested in appearances than edibility, often advising visiting dignitaries to dine with his epicurean ministers if they didn't share his tastes and himself wolfing down plain grub at odd hours, much in the manner of Caesar before him. His most significant contribution to gastronomy lay in his offer of a prize of

12,000 francs to anyone who could devise a method of preserving food for the use of troops on the march. The prize eventually was won by an obscure chemist or cook—biographers disagree—and inveterate tinkerer named either François or Nicholas Appert, who after fifteen years of dogged experimentation and flying glass perfected the hermetically sealed jar, thereby paving the way for the development of the tin can in England and such amenities of modern American life as Campbell's soups and Andy Warhol's paintings.

To return to Carême, he next turns up in the service of Antoine Marie Chamanes, comte de La Valette, an aide-de-camp to Napoleon reputed to have maintained one of France's finest tables; and, later, as executive chef in Talleyrand's kitchen, where he was to remain for twelve happy years.

Talleyrand was—by the consent of almost everyone but the sole pretender to gastronomic preeminence, Napoleon's archchancellor Jean-Jacques Cambacérès—the "finest fork" in the nation. A political survivor whose highest aspirations were "to give good dinners and keep well with women," he spent an hour each morning planning the evening's menu and set a table Carême was joyously to describe as being "furnished at once with grandeur and wisdom." If ever there was a meeting of minds, this was it: the man who later was to be called "the Cook of kings and King of cooks" and the ultimate connoisseur, the *amphitryon par excellence.* "Everything was ability, order, splendor," the great chef burbled. "Talent was happy there, and highly placed. . . . What great tableaux [were] created! Who has not seen them has seen nothing."

If the Carême-Talleyrand tableaux were impressive, one *beau geste* engineered by Cambarécès was hardly less so. At one of his modest soirées for fifty or sixty of the *crème de la crème,* carefully rehearsed lackeys "stumbled" on their way to the table, allowing a gargantuan Caspian sturgeon worth a king's ransom to flop ignominiously onto the floor. "Serve the *other* sturgeon," the host airily commanded, whereupon a leviathan that might have given pause to a Captain Ahab made its appearance.

France's leading *pâtissier* during the years of Carême's youth was a certain Avice, of whom little is known except that Carême revered him and, as Prosper Montagné expressed it, gave him "first place among the pastry cooks of that brilliant epoch." Whether Carême at any point established direct contact with Avice is questionable. "At that time," he recalled somewhat equivocally later in life, "Avice flourished in the realm of *pâtisserie*; his work served as my instruction. The knowledge of his procedures gave me courage, and I did all I could to follow him, but not to imitate him." At some point during his formative years he also appears to have absorbed various mysteries of the culinary art under the direct or indirect influence of the leading specialists of the day. ("It was under M. Richaut, the famous sauce cook of the house of Condé, that I learned the preparation of sauces . . . under the orders of M. Lasne that I learned the best part of cold buffet cookery, at the Elysée Napoléon under the auspices of Messrs. Robert and Laguipière that I learned the elegance of modern cookery and the renaissance of

Antonin Carême, the founder of la cuisine classique *and perhaps the greatest chef who ever lived, was born in Paris in 1784. He first trained as a pâtissier but went on to study the other culinary arts under the leading chefs of France. "The Cook of kings and the King of cooks" served Talleyrand, Tsar Alexander I, the future George IV of England, Lord Castlereagh, and Baron de Rothschild, but his greatest contribution to gastronomy lies in the books he wrote toward the end of his brilliant career. In them he stressed the importance of marketing, freshness of ingredients, kitchen organization, a systematic culinary orthography, and the relation of various courses to the whole.*

the art.") With all this and a dozen years of sovereignty in Talleyrand's kitchens behind him, he was probably the most accomplished cook in Christendom when he moved on to conquer new worlds.

His next stop was England, where he served as chef to the prince regent (the future George IV), who professed some alarm at the prodigality of the temptations set before him. Noting that it was "no concern" of his to curb the royal appetite, but his job to stimulate it, Carême returned to France and "that most, most alluring of French conversation" (conversation that presumably didn't include protestations that "You will kill me with a surfeit of food"), and from there to such prestigious kitchens as those of Tsar Alexander I (a notable gourmet who died of mushroom poisoning after Carême's departure), Lord Castlereagh, the court of Vienna, the Congress of Aix-la-Chapelle, and, finally, the baron de Rothschild, by then the successor to Talleyrand as France's leading epicure. After seven years with the financier, Carême rejected Rothschild's entreaties to remain at his post and retired to "humble lodgings" in Paris, there to produce "a comprehensive survey of the state of my profession at the present time." The work was to

The opulent tastes of the prince regent who became England's George IV are much in evidence at the Royal Pavilion he built in Brighton. The quasi-Chinese decor of the grand dining room (right) is repeated in the pavilion's well-equipped kitchen (left). The latter could boast of the most modern of cooking equipment—there were all manner of contrivances for roasting, baking, steaming, stewing, frying, and heating. But even these were not enough to induce the great Carême to remain in the monarch's employ. He found the royal majesty's tastes "too bourgeois"—and returned to France.

comprise five titles and eleven illustrated volumes. Accounts of his death differ. The more plausible have him expiring in his bed while dictating culinary notes to a daughter. Others would have it that he collapsed, sauté pan in hand, correcting a pupil's mishandling of *quenelles*. Whatever the manner of his going, he left behind a body of theoretical knowledge that his successors were to put to practical use by means of the Rumford range.

Throughout his career Carême's stated aims had been "delicacy, order, and economy"—the latter a seemingly startling consideration in view of the solvency of his employers, but one that was revolutionary in its time and since has been the linchpin of the French cuisine, as it is of every cuisine worth the name. Much as he might extol splendor and rhapsodize over "only the most sanitary and finest products [that] were employed" in Talleyrand's kitchens, splendiferous as his culinary productions were expected to be, he abhorred waste, and today's gastronomy in the more affluent nations is the poorer for not following his lead in this respect. (He also railed against the use of leftovers, doubtless because little of what *he* prepared went uneaten.)

Wisdom, order, economy, experience, excellence—these were the qualities Carême prized and, indeed, demanded. His disgust with the many cookbook authors who lacked his own understanding of the métier was monumental, and not even the hallowed Brillat-Savarin, whom he considered a provincial boor, escaped his wrath. Righteous indignation and boundless self-esteem fill the pages of his books. The redoubtable Cambacérès is contemptuously dismissed as a confessed eater of meatball pies (which on the face of it sounds like an indictable offense). Napoleon's exile on St. Helena is insupportable barbarism, not for political reasons but because the Little Corporal had nothing of interest to eat there but bananas. The mission of his art, he fervently believed, was to "serve as a foil to European diplomacy. . . . Good cooking," he added, "should strengthen the life of old societies."

To those who eat merely to live, Carême's fervent espousal of his cause may seem a trifle excessive. The right-minded among us, however, will recognize in his fulminations the missionary zeal of the embattled and incorruptible artist to whom the slightest compromise with truth as he saw it resulted in the death of the soul. His legacy was, above all, *Le Pâtissier Royal Parisien*, a book that, unlike any of its forerunners, stressed the importance of marketing, freshness of ingredients, kitchen organization, a systematic culinary orthography, and the relation of sauces, consommés, and hors d'oeuvres to the whole. From his drawings we know that his set pieces were incredibly detailed works in spun sugar—works that almost establish his claim to the supremacy of confectionery among the branches of architecture. From his simpler, more down-to-earth recipes it's obvious that the man also could cook.

By leaving the great chefs and *maîtres d'hotel* unemployed while creating a large class of *nouveaux riches*, the French Revolution paved the way for a spate of cookbooks and the rise of the restaurant. Cabarets had existed for some time and were quite popular well before the last quarter of the sixteenth century, when even royalty patronized such establishments as Le Mouton Blanc, the Innocent, the Harvard, Le Petit Diable, La Pomme de Pin (a hangout of Villon's and Rabelais's), Le Sabot, and La Corne. The fare served was hearty, substantial, and usually limited to a *table d'hôte*. The chief attractions, then as now (although the term "cabaret" has taken on a somewhat different coloration), were conviviality and the chance to rub elbows with the cele-

Pl. 30.

According to Carême, "The fine arts are five in number, to wit: painting, sculpture, poetry, music, architecture—whose main branch is confectionery." A glance at drawings he made for some of his incredibly detailed works in spun sugar (above) would seem to establish his claim that confectionery is architecture. Although these elaborate pièces montées *were usually inedible, recipes and other illustrations (left) prove Carême's gustatory genius.*

brated. The café, like the English coffeehouse, had come to prominence in the seventeenth century, after an enterprising Sicilian named Francisco Procopio opened the Café Procope, a coffeehouse-cum-ice-cream-parlor, in 1660—and inns and taverns had, of course, been around since the Middle Ages. Not even the term "restaurant," however, let alone anything that might be thought of as such today, existed.

In 1765 a soup vendor on the rue Bailleul hung a sign over his door to advise passers-by that "Boulanger sells magical restoratives ["*restaurants*"]. Little is known of Boulanger except that he seems not long thereafter to have tired of ladling out nothing but soups, however magical they may have been, and augmented his menu with a dish of sheep's feet in white sauce; a move that brought immediate litigation down on his head as the strictly controlled *traiteurs*, or eating-house keepers, the only licensed purveyors of "whole pieces" in sauce, strove to protect their threatened rights.

The case eventually went to the Parlement of Paris, with that august body decreeing that learned disquisition had established no precedent for sauced sheep's feet and—ah, those logical French!—that therefore the extremities in question were not a *ragout* as the civilized world understood the term and thus not illegal. The notoriety conferred on Boulanger by the proceedings sent all Paris flocking to his establishment to eat a dish that eventually made its way to the disappearing table of Louis XV. The monarch, however, didn't share the enthusiasm of his subjects. The dish's popularity soon waned and Boulanger's only lasting contribution to gastronomy remains his unwitting addition to its vocabulary.

Brillat-Savarin defines a restaurant as a place that offers "to the public an ever-ready feast, the dishes of which are served in separate portions, at fixed prices, at the request of each consumer." It is generally agreed that the first venture to meet these criteria was the Grand Taverne de Londres, which opened on the rue de Richelieu, probably in 1782, closed during the Revolution, and reopened toward the end of the Directoire. Its *patron* was Beauvilliers, a former household steward to the comte de Provence (later Louis XVIII) and *attaché extraordinaire* at court; a man who dressed to the nines, spoke five languages, possessed a phenomenal memory for names and faces, and who later in life was to write what Brillat-Savarin considered the greatest of all cookbooks. "He was the first," the sometime mayor of Belley wrote, "to combine an elegant dining room, smart waiters, and a choice cellar with superior cooking . . . during the two . . . occupations of Paris, in 1814 and 1815, vehicles of all nations were constantly at his door."

The *soigné* Beauvilliers was at the door too, complete with sword and ruffled shirt, to greet his clients in their own tongues and by name, however infrequently or long ago they had visited the place. A big spender himself, he treated his guests like the royalty they often were, impeccably observing the intricacies of protocol, offering discreet suggestions, and socking them with a staggering *addition* at meal's end. (Beauvilliers's elevated prices set the standard for the day. "To dine at the Café de Paris," the *Almanach des Gourmands* reported a few years later, "one needs to be a millionaire . . . [and] an English peer to dine at the Café Anglais." A fish at the celebrated Rocher de Cancale, the paper went on to say, "is worth its weight in 5-franc pieces.") Beauvilliers, who made and squandered several fortunes, appears to have died penniless in 1820.

In 1786 a signboard hoisted under the arcade of the Palais Royal signaled the opening of Aux Trois Frères Provençaux. The city's second restaurant of consequence, it had been founded by three clever entrepreneurs who, by various accidents of birth, happened not to be the siblings they advertised themselves to be. Nor did they hail from the

Midi, as claimed, but their establishment became famous for salt cod with garlic, which did, and as the training ground for several notable chefs of the nineteenth century. Before long these pioneers were joined by others: the fashionable Café Conti (later the Grand Véfour), Le Boeuf à la Mode (specializing in the pot roast that now bears that name), the Café de Chartres, Café Hardy, and Café Riche (a facetious maxim of the time had it that one must be "*riche* to dine *chez* Hardy and hardy to dine *chez* Riche"). Then there were Very's restaurant, with a menu of bewildering prolixity; the Café Tortoni, famed for its ices; the Petit Moulin, where the greatest of modern chefs, Escoffier, was to begin his career; the Rocher de Cancale, which specialized in fish and was owned by a man fittingly named Baleine ("whale"); the Café de Paris; and dozens, then hundreds, finally thousands of others.

With the rise of the restaurant a whole new breed of *bons vivants* came into being: the semiprofessional diner-out, the *amateur de gourmandisme* who brought his highest critical and appreciative faculties to bear on what was set before him. There was the elder Dumas, a famed host and salad maker who made a life's work of his *Grand Dictionnaire de la Cuisine*, a book his detractors (and they were legion) condemned as outdated even before the ink was dry on its pages. There

was the redoubtable Cambacérès of the splattered sturgeon, president of the Jury Dégustateur, the most powerful of the innumerable epicurean societies then being formed for the purpose of sampling and rating anonymously prepared dishes. There was Louis XVIII, who had his chops grilled in tiers of three, from which he extracted and ate only the succulent one in the middle.

But by far the most important gourmet was Brillat-Savarin, the portly small-town magistrate who had supported himself as a violin teacher while sitting out the Terror in New York, and who stuffed the pockets of his ill-fitting old-fashioned coats with the small game he would entrust to no one until it was sufficiently high. He was born in 1775, in Bugey, a region famed for its food and drink, and of a family of ravenous appetite and great staying power (his sister Pierrette is supposed to have died in her hundredth year, howling for dessert). He remained a lifelong bachelor but had a keen eye for the ladies, whom he found most alluring when their cheeks were full of food, and particularly for his cousin Juliette Récamier, Chateaubriand's mistress.

Brillat-Savarin's book, a work without precedent in postclassical Western literature, stunned contemporaries who had taken him for a dull-witted, gluttonous bumpkin. It mixed erudition, wit, and wisdom in a fashion never before—or possibly since—applied to gastronomy.

Two of Paris's more prestigious restaurants were the Café Riche and the Café Hardy—and according to a facetious maxim of the day, one needed to be "riche to dine chez Hardy and hardy to dine chez Riche." At left is the well-stocked kitchen (complete with fish tank) of the Café Riche. Below, diners at the Boeuf à la Mode may well be sampling the well-known pot roast dish that bears the restaurant's name. At right, the Café Procope, minus the philosophes, appears little changed in this nineteenth-century view of the establishment seen on page 116.

Combining philosophical meditations, linguistic, chemical, physiological, and psychological analysis, personal observations and anecdotes, trenchant aphorisms ("The discovery of a new dish does more for the happiness of mankind than the discovery of a star"), it broke further new ground with its high praise of bourgeois and provincial cookery. No aspect of the art of eating escaped his attention, and the reaction of thousands of readers was summed up by one early convert who described *The Physiology of Taste* as "a divine book, which illuminates the art of eating with the light of genius."

Others illuminated the art with varying amounts of candlepower. The wittiest and most influential of them was Grimod de La Reynière, who, despite the loss of both hands in his youth, wielded as fine a fork as was to be found in Paris. The founder of the Jury Dégustateur, he also was publisher of the *Almanach des Gourmands*, the first journal of gastronomy. Highly opinionated and usually right, La Reynière was a punctilious diner, a mercilessly exacting critic, and a deft composer of such epigrams as "A well-made sauce will make even an elephant or a grandfather palatable." He and sixteen colleagues unfailingly dined each Wednesday at the Rocher de Cancale.

Neither Brillat-Savarin nor La Reynière, who also concerned himself with middle-class cooking and, more singularly, made himself the foremost advocate of the Italian-derived sauté, was concerned with recipes per se. Others were. Viard's *Le Cuisinier Imperial* appeared in 1806 and went through various editions—and politically prudent changes of title —during the course of the century. Its major innovations were its recipes for curries (which were then very much in vogue in England and France as both countries contended for supremacy in India), tomatoes, and potatoes.

The restaurateur Beauvilliers, opportunistically a proselyte of the English cookery that became fashionable in France after Waterloo, introduced his readers to such exotica as *rostbif*, *biftek*, *wouelche rabette*, *plumbuting*, and *machpotetesse* in his *L'Art du Cuisinier*, even while a transplanted compatriot, Louis-Eustache Ude, was familiarizing the victors with *la cuisine française*. Another Louis-Eustache, surnamed Audot, published *The Country and City Cookbook*, bestowing additional legitimacy on provincial cookery, and by mid-century the thrifty Gallic homemaker was up to her *bain-marie* in works on the use of cheaper cuts and leftovers—a circumstance that must have had Carême and La Reynière whirling in their graves.

The mid-nineteenth century was notable, gastronomically speaking, for the birth of two men who were to reign supreme over the international version of *la dolce vita* several decades later. Auguste Escoffier, a blacksmith's son, first saw the light of day in an obscure village in the Maritime Alps in 1846. César Ritz was born in 1850 in a comparably unprepossessing setting in Switzerland, near the Simplon Pass, the not-altogether-welcome son of a peasant couple already burdened with a dozen get. Escoffier was to become the finest chef since Carême and perhaps the greatest who ever lived. Ritz, destined to be the hotelier par excellence, eventually would make his name synonymous with the good life. The world they were to conquer was a changing one. The old order was on the wane, new money abounded, and *arrivistes* in search of a life-style of their own demanded new pleasures.

Les Rêves d'un Gourmand.

ALMANACH
DES GOURMANDS,
SERVANT DE GUIDE DANS LES MOYENS
DE FAIRE EXCELLENTE CHÈRE.

PAR UN VIEIL AMATEUR.

SIXIÈME ANNÉE,

Contenant plusieurs articles qu'il importe aux Amphitryons, aux convives, et surtout aux Gourmands, de lire et de méditer; des Découvertes importantes pour les Gourmets; quelques Chapitres de Morale et de Métaphysique gourmandes; des Recettes inédites et curieuses; un petit Traité des Liaisons, des Braises et des Coulis; des considérations sur les Progrès de l'art du Four, sur plusieurs objets d'Economie domestique, et sur quelques Marchés de Paris; des Poésies et des Chansons gourmandes; la Petite Revue de l'année 1808, formant la Sixième Promenade d'un Gourmand dans Paris, etc. etc. etc.

Anseris ante ipsum magni jecur, anseribus par Altilis, et flavi dignus ferro Meleagri Fumat aper.
Juvénal, Sat. v. vers. 114.

DE L'IMPRIMERIE DE CELLOT.

A PARIS,
Chez MARADAN, Libraire, rue des Grands-Augustins, n°. 9.
M. DCCC. VIII.

Both Ritz and Escoffier were peculiarly suited to the temper of the times. Unlike the great chefs and *maîtres d'hôtel* of the past, neither went into private service in the noble houses. Instead, the twelve-year-old Escoffier was sent to an uncle's restaurant in Nice, where he was put to work as a scullion, while Ritz began his career as an apprentice wine steward in an inconsequential hotel. Paris, of course, with its multiplicity of fine restaurants, its glitter, and its glamour, was then the ultimate goal of every provincial of any ambition in the trade. Both young men soon turned up there.

Both were recognized—and recognized each other—as brilliant men of unusual promise and similar temperament; temperament, moreover, that accorded well with that of the many *nouveaux riches* to whom they catered. *Arrivistes* themselves and richly patinated with acquired snobbery, they were men of imposing appearance with a marked talent for showmanship. (Even Ritz's name could only have worked to his advantage. Ritz!—no other syllable in the world's languages is conceivable for the panache the man came to represent. A Tin-pan Alley lyri-

cist might pore through the world's telephone books and not improve on "Putting on the Ritz.") When Ritz gravitated to Monte Carlo as the newly appointed manager of the Grand Hotel, it was only natural that he invite Escoffier to join him there as chef. It was the start of a partnership that eventually would shape the style of an era that posterity would one day wistfully look back to as *la belle époque*.

It was an era of mobility, with fast, magnificently appointed trains smoothly transporting Europe's—and America's—leisured from spa to spa, race to race, hunt to hunt, regatta to regatta, casino to casino, and capital to capital, eating superbly en route and magnificently on arrival. And as they moved, Ritz's burgeoning hotel empire spread to accommodate them. Baden-Baden, Monte Carlo, Frankfurt, Rome, Biarritz, Madrid—almost wherever they went, this indefatigable entrepreneur was there before them, seeing to it that they could rest assured of living and eating in the style to which, in large part thanks to him, they had become accustomed.

Only London seemed beyond Ritz's grasp, for the Englishman at home was notoriously a different animal from the Englishman abroad. On the Continent this curious phlegmatic creature stayed at the poshest hotels, unflappably picked up tabs of alarming magnitude at the most fashionable restaurants. On his native turf, however, he sequestered himself in his club or his home, leaving such raffish eating houses as Kettner's, Simpson's, and Romano's to his social inferiors and gorging behind closed doors on what Sydney Smith called "barbarian Stone-

César Ritz (far right), the nineteenth century's hotelier par excellence, was born in Switzerland in 1850. He began his career at the tender age of fifteen, shortly thereafter gravitating to Paris, with its fine patisseries (above) and glamorous atmosphere. Ritz was an impresario of the first order, a master of protocol, and a stickler for detail. All the hotels and restaurants that he established (his Paris operation is depicted at right) bore the stamp of his magnetic personality. Indeed, his very name has come to connote elegance and panache.

henge masses of meat" and another dyspeptic observer remembered with "an inward shudder."

Still, when the theatrical impresario Richard D'Oyly Carte argued that his countrymen would come out if only they had an establishment worth coming out for, and that Ritz and Escoffier (whose talents had impressed him at Baden-Baden) were just the men to create such an establishment, Ritz and Escoffier were off to London. Their expatriation produced the Savoy Hotel, an institution without precedent anywhere in Europe, whose most splendiferous hostelries suddenly looked like medieval country inns by comparison. The place boasted no fewer than seventy bathrooms—sixty-six more than its closest competitor—and appointments worthy of Europe's royal palaces. No patron's demand for personal attention, however idiosyncratic, failed to be gratified forthwith. Every facet of the operation was attended by a punctilio worthy of Versailles in the time of the Sun King. And, of course, there was the grand dining salon, where evening dress was *de rigueur*, and where the likes of Lady Randolph Churchill, the duchess of Marlborough, and the prince of Wales dined on frogs' legs that the great Escoffier was pleased to call *Cuisses des Nymphes à l'Aurore*.

Escoffier was to spend most of his working career in London, first

HOTEL RITZ
PLACE VENDOME PARIS

LA SALLE RÉGENCE

Le plus artistique des Restaurants. ✻ Rendez-vous de l'élite de la Société parisienne et étrangère.

HOTEL RITZ	GRILL ROOM
Le plus artistique et le plus confortable des hôtels modernes, comportant les derniers perfectionnements.	Le grill-room récemment ouvert est devenu un lieu de rendez-vous pour les déjeuners simples, les diners et les soupers.
Chaque chambre à coucher comporte une salle de bains.	On y trouve aussi un bar américain.

Five o'clock le plus select.

at the Savoy and later at the Carlton, also operated by Ritz. In the course of that career he engineered still another of the periodic revolutions undergone by French gastronomy throughout its history. Following a precept set forth by Brillat-Savarin, he arranged his courses in a progression from the substantial to the light, orchestrating the entire meal around a central theme, with soups functioning as "an overture . . . [to indicate] what is to be the dominant phrase of the melody throughout." Substituting the new service *à la russe* for the old style of loading the table with an ostentatious display of the whole meal, he punctuated his courses with changes of wine in lieu of the customary sherbets, drastically cut down on the number of covers served, and did away altogether with the indiscriminate, catch-as-catch-can nature of dining that had followed the same basic pattern since the Renaissance.

124

The great chef Auguste Escoffier (left) was to revolutionize
the French gastronomical tradition. He likened a formal dinner to a symphony, stressing
that both consisted of contrasting movements but contained an
underlying theme. In addition,
he arranged his courses in a progression from the substantial to
the light. This new style of service was to become the model for
the twentieth-century banquet
(far left). The contributions of
Escoffier were monumental, but
French gastronomy is the sum
of many parts—it is equally indebted to the Les Halles asparagus seller seen directly below,
and to Mme Harel, whose statue
(below, right) commemorates her
discovery of Camembert.

After sixty-two years in the kitchen, Escoffier retired, heavy with
honors, to write (his *Guide Culinaire* remains a classic). He had won
the praises of the crowned heads of Europe (to Kaiser Wilhelm II, who
called him "the Emperor of Chefs" and asked, "How can I repay you?"
he tartly replied, "By giving us back Alsace-Lorraine"), radically
changed the gastronomy of a continent and, with Ritz, made wine connoisseurship something much like a religion among upper-class Englishmen. He had also set the standards by which the Western world still
measures the good life.

France had produced other great chefs and countless other figures
of culinary and gastronomic importance. There was Laguipière, for
one, whom Carême revered and who died during the Napoleonic
retreat from Russia. There was Chandelier, another of Carême's gods,
faithful to the Little Corporal in good times and bad, and the master
pastrycook Lebeau, the designer of Bonaparte's *pièces montées* until
Carême replaced him. Dugléré held sway at the Café Anglais in the
mid-nineteenth century and wrote what *La Vie Parisienne* termed "a
page of history" when he served dinner one memorable evening to a
party comprised of the king and crown prince of Prussia, Bismarck, and
the tsar and tsarevich of Russia. There was the great *poissonier* Mar-
guery (whose epitaph, written by an American in Paris, was, "His sole
goes marching on"); Montagné, who won the ribbon of the Légion
d'Honneur for his cooking and the gratitude of generations for *Larousse Gastronomique*; Mère Poulard, who was renowned throughout France for the omelets she turned out of a long-handled pan at
Mont Saint-Michel; Close, the "inventor" of *pâté de foie gras*; and Mme
Harel, whose statue in Vimoutiers, Normandy, commemorates her discovery of Camembert cheese.

The list is indefinitely extendable, but Carême and Brillat-Savarin,
Escoffier and Ritz, Beauvilliers and Grimod de La Reynière—these,
with the slightly incongruous Rumford, were the salient figures of a
century whose gastronomic like, to the impoverishment of future generations, probably will never be seen again.

8

The Other Cuisine

If there is anything we are serious about, it is neither religion nor learning, but food.

Lin Yutang
My Country and My People

IT IS THE UNSHAKABLE CONVICTION of most Frenchmen that no other cuisine exists but their own. Pressed on the point, an unusually liberal Frenchman may grudgingly concede that, yes, perhaps one might call what the Chinese have developed another cuisine—*the* other cuisine. The clear implication, though, is that it's not a cuisine to be taken seriously, but one of those aberrations, like not speaking French, to which backward peoples seem to be subject.

The fact is that the Chinese had a cuisine, and an extremely sophisticated one at that, when the Gauls and Franks were still gnawing bark and trying to make bread of mud, oxblood, and coarse flour. There is clear evidence that both cooking and eating were elaborately codified, infinitely subtle pursuits by the time of Confucius' birth in the sixth century B.C.

Perhaps nowhere else has a cuisine been shaped as fully by societal, religious, and topographical exigencies as has the cuisine of China, a land that has been overpopulated and fuel-poor for centuries. If the Frenchman will sample almost anything edible in his eternal quest for new gustatory sensations, the Chinese will, of necessity, consume anything (without the qualifier) he can safely ingest. Dogs, cats, rats, snakes, grasshoppers (euphemistically called "brushwood shrimps"), silkworms, grubs, and other unwary Chinese—all these and many other items morally or aesthetically repugnant to Westerners have at one time or another played more or less prominent roles in the Chinese diet, and most still do.

Moreover, the very texture of Chinese food has been determined by culinary techniques shaped by an age-old, acute shortage of slow-burning fuels. Despite Lamb's engaging *Dissertation on Roast Pig*, and the distinctive roast pork ubiquitous in Chinese restaurants in the West (probably better known to Americans than to most Chinese, who, when they have eaten it at all, have bought it ready-cooked from an establishment whose sales volume justified the extensive use of fuel needed to roast it properly), the roast, as Westerners conceive it, is unknown in

Only 15 percent of mainland China is arable, and those acres have been intensively cultivated for millennia to feed the world's most populous nation. Dependent since predynastic times upon a single major crop—rice—the Chinese have suffered severely with each crop failure. The scroll painting detail opposite recreates those lean times: emaciated peasants collapse from malnourishment (foreground) as others, slightly better off, beg for food and fuel (center left).

China and doubtless would be accorded much the same reception there that sea slugs, lizards, and similar Chinese delicacies are given here.

Conversely, the Chinese, with few milk-producing animals, are repelled by dairy foods. "They especially loathe butter and cheese," one early twentieth-century observer wrote, "and speak of the foreigner smelling like the Mongol—an odour which they say is the result of those two articles of diet." Indeed, the adult Chinese digestive system seems unable to assimilate milk; a result, the food historian Reay Tannahill hypothesizes, of a millennial need to cultivate every square yard of arable land—thus eliminating the possibility of stock-raising.

The early course of Chinese gastronomy has yet to be traced. Millet appears to have been the first cultivated grain and the soybean —an extremely versatile and nutritious source of protein and a notable rejuvenator of the soil in which it grows—the first legume. These, with rice (introduced from the Indus Valley, probably around 3000 B.C.), wheat, and barley, were the staple, "sacred" crops according to the putative writings of the emperor Shen Nung—who, if he ever really existed, lived sometime closer to 2700 B.C. than to the Paleolithic era to which legend assigns him. The pig, the major meat source throughout recorded Chinese history, was domesticated some five thousand years ago. There appears, however, to be some evidence that meat was in short supply (and that laws were enacted for the conservation of game) by around 1000 B.C.—a condition that conceivably accounts for the northward spread of Indian Buddhism and its vegetarian tenets several centuries later.

Buddhism doubtless had a somewhat limiting effect on the Chinese diet, although it should be emphasized that it's hard to separate cause and effect where the diffusion of the religion and the spread of vegetarianism are concerned. Mankind has a curious way of curbing its carnivorous tendencies when there's no meat around. It also might be noted that the Chinese Buddhist, unlike the Indian, long has tended to gloss over prohibitions against the consumption of flesh, at least when he has found it available.

Confucianism was another matter. Confucius himself may or may not have been the dedicated gourmet some food enthusiasts would have us believe he was. Little light is shed on the subject one way or the

"What smell is this, so strong and good?" asks a verse in the Shih-ching, or "Book of Songs," China's earliest extant text. The answer—at least in 600 B.C., the century in which the songs were compiled—might well have been mutton, for pens of sheep were a common sight at the time (and an inspiration for the clay model seen at lower left). In addition to rice, the early Chinese harvested millet, wheat, and barley —a task for which the young girl at right is well equipped.

other by his own assertion: "With coarse rice to eat, with water to drink, and my bended arm for a pillow—I still have joy in the midst of these things." Elsewhere he insists that rice "must be polished" and, short of outright drunkenness, puts no limit on wine intake.

Whether Confucius himself ate very grandly or not, he did set forth gastronomic precepts that convey a clear idea of the sophistication of Chinese dining five and a half centuries before the dawn of the Christian era—a sophistication it almost certainly had attained some time before he recorded its underlying principles. In his *Analects*, Confucius makes abundantly evident the esteem in which rice was then held, noting that it must be cleaned and washed before cooking and not have been exposed to the debilitating effects of heat and dampness. Meat, he added, must be finely minced and fish kept fresh. Improperly cooked or unseasonable foods were to be avoided. Though no restrictions were put on the consumption of meat (so long as it wasn't bought dried at the market), its quantity was never to "exceed the proportion of the rice" and not make one's breath "smell of meat rather than rice."

To be sure, most of these rules, like the dietary laws of the Jews, had to do more with hygienic than aesthetic considerations. Since pork was the staple meat, for example, the stricture that it be finely minced was simply a precaution against contracting trichinosis. On the other hand, there is nothing in Hebraic dietary injunctions to parallel the Confucian prohibition of meat "served without its proper sauce," inappropriately seasoned, or "crookedly cut."

Taoism, too, made its contribution to Chinese gastronomy. While Confucius preached a doctrine of stylized elegance, his contemporary Lao-tse called for a return to simple, frugal living and a closer rapport with nature, the latter to be achieved in part by eating only the tenderest young shoots and vegetables and retaining their basic characteristics in the process of preparing them for the table. If they could be eaten raw, so much the better; if they required cooking they were to be cooked as lightly as possible.

Here then was a case of practical expediency being given ritual form. Both Confucius' advocacy of artful slicing and Lao-tse's esteem for crisp, undercooked greens had to do at bottom with a dwindling fuel supply caused by a population explosion on the Yangtze River plain. As the forests beyond that fertile expanse disappeared (and with them the game they had sheltered, making a modified form of vegetarianism necessary if not altogether palatable), a cuisine of oven-baking, spit-roasting, and slow-simmered stews was out of the question. With fires stoked with such highly combustible but quickly consumed materials as straw, dried leaves, shocks, and the like, what the Chinese needed was a cuisine that enabled them to cook complete dishes in the shortest possible time. Out of that need came the Oriental technique of stir-frying.

In principle the stir-fry is little different from the sauté devised by the Italians when their fuel supply ran short. Whereas the Italian slices his *scaloppine* very thin, however, he still allows it to cover a sizable portion of the sauté pan. The Chinese, in an even bigger hurry, not only cuts his meats (and vegetables) even more thinly, but in much

smaller pieces, often producing fine dice or the shreds the French call *julienne* in the process, thereby carrying a good idea to its logical conclusion. With the several elements of his dish whittled down to fine dimensions, with a thin-bodied vessel (the *wok*) that transmits heat to food with virtually no delay, and with ingredients added in a rapid succession dictated by the relative cooking times they require, minimal cooking is needed to reproduce a fully orchestrated, piping-hot meal whose various components maintain their individual identities while blending into a harmonious whole.

Harmony is essential to Chinese cookery but, as in Chinese painting, harmony is the offspring of contrast: soft and hard, chewy and crisp, thick and thin, clear and opaque. In no other cuisine, save possibly the Japanese, has the Chinese realization of the importance of color been even remotely approached—and in no other cuisine have what a painter might call the "tactile values" figured so prominently in the composition of both the single dish and the full meal.

Another fundamental tenet of Chinese gastronomy was fully established at least as early as the fourth century B.C. and demonstrates the subtlety of which the art was then capable. This held that there are five basic taste sensations (sweet, sour, briny, hot, and bitter) and that the

Gastronomy in China, a matter of aesthetic as well as gustatory concern in a society ruled by aesthetes, was to become as regulated and systematized as the nation's social order. In the sixteenth-century painting below, ladies of the imperial court engage in their customary leisure activities—which include the preparation of the emperor's tea (center left). The seventeenth-century brush holder at left is banded with a depiction in high relief of a group of scholars picnicking in a pavilion.

well-planned menu takes all of them into account; a formulation, simple as it may sound, that was never independently articulated in the West.

While stir-frying was, and remains, the basic Chinese cooking technique, it wasn't the only technique in use. Noodles and rice, the staple starches of the north and south respectively, along with cabbage, spinach, and other leaf vegetables, required boiling. This, as it happened, could be accomplished quickly over unregulated heat, as could the steaming of fish, dumplings, and bread. (Baked bread, while not altogether unknown, has been a rarity throughout Chinese history; steamed breads have been eaten extensively, however.) In one technical *tour de force*, crystal chicken, a whole fowl required precisely one minute of cooking time.

Just as the nature of his food had been determined by the cooking methods he had perforce to employ, the universal eating implement of the Chinese was shaped by the nature of his food. Confronted with an array of finely cut meats and vegetables and a bowl of rice or noodles, he found that two slender, tapering sticks were uniquely fitted to the job at hand. Literally an extension of his fingers—and almost as sensitive—they enabled him fastidiously to pluck dainty morsels from a delicately perfumed sauce at a time when the West was up to its collective elbows in noisome gravy. By far the most graceful of the surprisingly few eating tools with which man has equipped himself, a well-handled pair of chopsticks makes for an exercise in dexterity beside which the use of a knife and fork resembles a slapstick clash of arms. With his chopsticks the early Chinese, almost from birth, could manipulate a single grain of rice or reduce a whole carp to bare bones.

The Chinese poor ate as the poor everywhere have eaten since time immemorial—poorly. In the best of times they subsisted on rice or noo-

dles, garnishing these plain boiled staples with whatever they could scrounge. In times of war or crop failure, famine was rife. Needless to say, the poor Chinese knew no more of gastronomy, "the art or science of eating well," than the average working rhinoceros knows of Mozart. (Eating, incidentally, might be termed the employment of most living species except man, among whose number only the infant and the restaurant reviewer make a vocation of the ingestion of food.) For the overwhelming majority of Chinese since the depletion of the forests, just eating—let alone eating well—has involved a struggle to keep in productive shape the meager 15 per cent or so of their land that is arable; a struggle that necessitated husbanding every scrap of waste, including human waste products, for fertilizer, and the laborious business of dredging canals and creeks each winter for the richly organic accumulated muck on their bottoms.

For those who could afford it, gastronomy was perhaps the principal adornment of an eminently civilized life. A bowl of chicken soup might be the universal panacea to the proverbial Jewish mother, but to the Chinese epicure it was a piece of artistry to be considered on its own terms. Served in a translucent porcelain bowl hardly thicker than an eggshell, with fragrant petals floating on its surface, it was above all an object of contemplation, but one that by the grace of heaven and a good cook did as much for the inner man as for the higher faculties.

Each dish served at a Chinese banquet was expected to be as delicious as it was exquisite. A platter of cold meats, for example, might be a stunning work of *trompe l'oeil* that at first glance passed for a pheasant in full plumage, but each of its illusory elements had to be unadulterated and not just edible but delectable. Radishes, cucumbers, and fruits were cut in shapes that spoke a language of their own to the initiate, and casseroles were arranged to resemble jewel boxes or even costly fabrics. One of these, a tender vegetarian dish said to have been favored by toothless dowager empresses of the Ch'ing dynasty, is described by its name as "brocadelike."

A formal banquet might comprise anywhere from fifty to more

For China's upper classes, the art of eating well was a fusion of all the other arts. Thus, the Yüan dynasty painting at top left—entitled Whiling Away the Summer—*inevitably includes a section (left rear) devoted to brewing tea and to stir-frying over a brazier. The glazed porcelain syrup ewer at left, the lotus-shaped cup above, and the Ming dynasty bowl at right with its sculpted figures of the Eight Immortal Poets are additional examples of the frequency with which China's greatest artists applied their talents to the decoration of mundane serving vessels.*

than a hundred dishes, from which guests were expected to choose whatever tidbits tickled their fancy. Individual dishes ranged from the simplicity of grilled meats (which in no way resembled the Neanderthal cuts of today's American backyard barbecue) to such complex affairs as *yi p'ing kuo,* a Ming dynasty casserole of chicken, duck, dried shrimp, dried sea cucumber, shark's fin, ham, doves' eggs, water chestnuts, cabbage, green onion, and ginger. (Since the ghastly experiences undergone during the Middle Ages, the Western world has been notably reticent about mixing seafoods with meats, such exceptions as *vitello tonnato, paella,* and shad roe with bacon notwithstanding. The Chinese, on the other hand, have no difficulty in concocting palatable dishes from seemingly incongruous elements, a circumstance with which their quick cookery has had much to do. Slowly simmering a fish together with, say, a rump of beef—a common form of insanity in medieval Europe—can only work to the detriment of both ingredients, but such Chinese combinations, properly prepared, as ham and abalone, pork and eel, beef with oyster sauce, or even carp in mutton broth are unfailingly successful.)

Tea, which originated in India, reached China in the third century A.D. but did not come into widespread use until sometime during the T'ang dynasty. Five more centuries were to elapse before the English acquired a like passion for this most mild of stimulants. Thereafter, tea-tasting sessions, such as the one being conducted at left for two Occidental merchants, were to become commonplace. By the nineteenth century, tea leaves—and such accoutrements of the tea ceremony as the brilliantly colored Ming porcelainware at upper right—were China's principal export commodities.

The Chinese banquet—or any reasonably varied meal—hardly conformed to Western notions of progression and symmetry. Sweets or sweetened drinks were consumed at various stages of the action, as were soups, to refresh or cleanse the palate. Because it was signified by a written character that also meant "surplus" or "more," fish was traditionally the last item eaten. Desserts per se were unknown, as any Occidental might deduce from the short shrift given them by Chinese restaurants today, and rice, in several subtly inflected varieties, was to the meal what bread is in the West.

Games of skill and chance enlivened the proceedings during the course of a formal dinner. Despite Confucius' dictum (itself the product of some confused experiences) that "one should not become confused by overdrinking," the evening often would become riotously bibulous—except during the early years of the T'ang dynasty, when drinking was restricted to a rather solemn postprandial ritual. Or so it was by right-minded subjects, but not by Li Po, a renowned poet and monumental lush who headed up a hard-drinking group called "the Eight Immortals of the Wine Cup." Li turned out to be as mortal as the rest of us when, in "the rapture of drinking and wine's dizzy joy," he tried to embrace the moon (as it was reflected in an ornamental pool) and drowned.

Li and Confucius weren't the only ones who found their rice wine hard to handle. The Venetian Marco Polo discovered that "it makes one drunk sooner than any other wine."

Impressed as he may have been with what he drank—and he had more than fifty wines to choose from—Polo was dazzled even more by the river port of Hangchow, its general magnificence and its bustling fish market. Both an international trade nexus and a haven for refugees from the Mongol invaders, the city had been the capital of the Southern Sung dynasty during the century and a half before his arrival there and was in its heyday the Venice of the Orient and gastronomic capital of the known universe.

Set amidst rivers and lakes and within easy reach of both wooded mountains and the sea, Hanchow reaped a bounteous harvest of local and imported edibles. For centuries the merchants of the Indies and the Near East had traded pepper and other spices, sugar, fruits, and almonds for Chinese goods. By Polo's time, the city abounded in culinary delicacies. Local game, freshwater and marine fish, domestic geese and ducks—these and more could be had for pittances. Oysters were the fare of the poor and ginger, worth almost its weight in gold in Europe, was a drug on the market (in the next century Friar Odoric was to marvel at "three hundred pounds of ginger for less than a groat" and geese "as fat as fat can be" that sold for the same price).

In this cosmopolitan atmosphere restaurants and specialized shops for take-out foods proliferated almost as rapidly as the population, with various establishments (many of them run by Chinese Moslems, who were also the leading butchers) famed for such house specialities as fish soup, suckling pig cooked in ashes, honey fritters, shrimp pies, tripe, bean curd, smoked duck, soy soup, and shellfish. Quick-snack stands sold deep-fried wraplings much like the spring rolls known to Westerners today, and street vendors hawked their wares to passers-by. Caterers were in great demand and usually produced the elaborate dinners few hosts could turn out in their own kitchens. With its polyglot population and imported delicacies, the metropolis offered to those who could afford them a wide variety of fine rices and an eclectic cuisine drawn from the various regional styles of cookery: the sweet-and-sour dishes and subtle mushrooms of Honan to the north; the richly sauced seafoods of Canton on the South China Sea; the fiery stir-fries of Hunan and Szechuan in the interior; the imperial style of Peking; the honeyed corned ham of Yunnan; the hot-pots of the Mongols. And, of course, there were the teahouses, specializing in such variously scented, delicately tinted, and fancifully named brews as "Eyebrows of Longevity," "Dragon's Whiskers," and "Fragrant Forest."

Although the Chinese harbor some proprietary notions of the origin of tea and some exaggerated ideas of its antiquity, the plant was indigenous to India, probably didn't reach China until the third century A.D., and didn't become that country's national beverage until the eighth century. Curiously, however, the Indians never have been great tea drinkers, preferring instead milk, whey, syrups, and fruit juices.

As was the case with the Chinese, Arabs, and Jews, Indian gastronomy has been largely a matter of bending religious precepts to fit practical exigencies and sound hygienic practices. The sacred cow, for example, wasn't sanctified until some time after it became apparent to the Aryans, who settled in India in the second millennium B.C., that even though native Indian cattle weren't notable milk producers, slaughtering them for their meat was far less profitable than keeping them alive. Later, common sense became religious doctrine, the idea having developed by around 1000 B.C. that to eat the beef one's forebears hadn't been able to enjoy was to do violence to their memory. Still later, the doctrine of transmigration of souls, a basic tenet of the major indigen-

136

In the eighteenth-century engraving at lower left, Chinese fishermen employ trained cormorants to harvest fish from the still waters of a mountain lake. Restrictive collars prevent these large diving birds, cousins of the pelican, from swallowing more than a fraction of their catch. Fish—along with such staple grains as barley and rice— also figured prominently in the Indian diet. For both religious and economic reasons, Indian cuisine tends to the vegetarian— and this emphasis on fruits and vegetables is evident in the Persian miniature at right, which shows Shah Jahangir, fourth of the Mogul emperors, offering a variety of drinks and dishes to a royal guest seated to his left.

ous Indian religions, militated heavily against the consumption of meat, although an occasional hungry farmer stuck with a barren cow might transgress the injunction. Aside from the cow's greater importance as a source of dairy foods than of meat, however, another practical consideration worked to spare it from the butcher's knife: cattle were large animals and meat that wasn't immediately consumed couldn't be kept in the hot Indian climate—a circumstance the clergy was quick to recognize and deal with by devising a taboo against unclean foods. (It might also be noted that the climate wasn't in any case conducive to a heavy intake of meat.)

As in China, millet, wheat, barley, and rice were the staple grains from earliest antiquity, although rice was better suited to the monsoon-swept south and the others to the cooler, drier north. The lentil, while not nearly as versatile as the ubiquitous soybean of Chinese cookery, was, and remains, India's chief legume. These staples were

augmented by peas, beans, sugarcane, and such fruits as mangoes, plantains, jackfruit, coconuts, pomegranates, and tamarinds. Edward Lear's delightful nonsense notwithstanding, no early pumpkins blew on the coast of Coromandel, but foreign traders abounded there and on the Malabar coast, bringing with them the nutmeg, cloves, and mace of Indonesia and the milder spices of the Near East. In combination with native ginger, cardamom, pepper, rice, fish, and vegetables, these imported elements were to provide the basis for the South Indian cuisine.

To the northwest, Indian cookery was influenced by (and in turn influenced) the Persians, Greeks, and various central Asian peoples,

The Moguls, who conquered India from the north in the sixteenth century, brought a number of native Persian dishes with them. These included the skewered meat kebabs that are, with curries, a prime feature of Indian cuisine. This illustration, from a seventeenth-century edition of the Ramayana, *shows a kebab roast (center), culmination of the hunt seen at far right.*

while faint echoes of Chinese gastronomy reached the east coast and, in the south, reciprocal influences passed between India and Malaysia. Cooking styles varied from region to region, but *ghee*, or clarified butter, a relatively durable substance, was the universal cooking fat, and, like the Chinese, Indians everywhere (or at least those who lived above the subsistence level), adding astringency to the five fundamental sapors of China, built their meals around the concept of contrasting taste sensations.

While the poorer Indian struggled along, cooking whatever he could come by in crude vegetable oils, the well-to-do feasted, secure in their faith that even unclean foods would be purified if cooked in *ghee*. Some idea of the ultimate elaboration of high-class Indian gorging is conveyed by the ten-day-long festival of *Desehra*, a ritual observance of Rama's defeat of Ravana that evolved into a curious gustatory equivalent of the Christian carol *The Twelve Days of Christmas*. The festivities began modestly enough, with *payasam*, a rice-based sweet as the first day's *pièce de résistance*. With each succeeding day, however, there would be a reprise of the previous day's menu, which would be augmented with an entirely new and successively more impressive *carte du jour*. By the tenth day there would be a mind-bending array of sweet and savory rice dishes, yogurts, soups, cakes, curries, chutneys, dumplings, breads, pancakes, and vegetable *dhals*, or purees. Mogul blowouts, unfettered by the proscription of meats (except pork), would feature lamb *biryanis*, curries, *kebabs*, and even whole sheep, stuffed with pilaf, chickens, and hard-cooked eggs and braised in *ghee*. Halvahs, honeyed pastries, cooling sherbets, rosewater, fruits, and sweetened curds and yogurts pleasantly counterbalanced the fattiness of lamb and mutton, and it seems safe to say a good time was had by all.

During the Elizabethan era a traveler in the "Kingdome of Japonica" noted that the Japanese "delighte not much in fleshe, but they lyve for the most parte with herbes, fyshe, barley and ryce: which thynges are their chieffe nowrishments." What was true then was true centuries

Never in its long history has the mountainous Japanese archipelago been obliged to import rice, but this self-sufficiency has been achieved only through backbreaking toil in flooded hillside paddies (right). No other cuisine puts as much emphasis on presentation as does the Japanese, which in part accounts for the care lavished upon the lacquered serving tray at left.

before the birth of Christ and is still essentially true today. Influenced at first by the cookery of coastal China, less directly by the Mongol hot-pot (more or less duplicated in the Japanese *shabu-shabu*, named onomato-poetically for the sound allegedly made by boiling broth), by Portuguese innovations of the sixteenth century and, to a lesser extent, by the arrival of American carnivores in the nineteenth, the Japanese combined an essentially vegetarian, rice-based diet with their native seafoods to create the most exquisite of the world's cuisines; a cuisine characterized by extreme restraint, freshness, tact, and refinement.

If the Chinese were great conservators of fuel, the Japanese were even more so. In no other cuisine is such extensive use made of raw foods and in no other, the Chinese included, are cooked foods cooked so lightly. As Daniel J. Meloy, a longtime observer of Japanese life, has noted, "... the essence of Japanese cuisine [is] the quality of being *assari*—plain simple, straightforward, even spartan, but with delicacy."

To the Japanese, even more punctilious than the Chinese, the presentation of a meal and the quality of its ambience is at least as significant as the food itself. From the steamed hand towels proffered after diners seat themselves, cross-legged and unshod on *tatami* mats, to the disposable chopsticks (much lighter than the Chinese variety) with which the food is eaten, each appurtenance is chosen with an eye both to its fitness for its particular function and its presentability as an object worthy of formal admiration.

After observing that the Japanese had "strong wine and rack distilld of ryce, of which they will sometimes drinke largely, especially at their feasts and meetings," our Elizabethan informant adds, "As concernynge another drinke, they take great delighte in water mingled with

Because Japanese cooks eschew strong seasonings and sauces, there is no way of masking the taste of overage produce. As a result, all foods must be consumed at peak freshness. Fish, being cleaned at left above, are often served raw, and fowl are diced, skewered, and then roasted briefly over a charcoal fire.

The making and serving of tea (right above) is a ritual that inculcates many aspects of Japanese aesthetics. So comforting is this practice, in fact, that natives often travel with their own tea implements. One such set, pictured below, includes a tall lacquer tea canister, a footed bowl, and a bamboo whisk.

a certain powder which is very pretiouse, which they call *chia*."

"*Chia*" (derived from the Cantonese *chah*) is, of course, tea, whose service and consumption, a strictly regulated rite in China, became something like a full-fledged religion in Japan in the sixteenth century. The brew had been introduced into the islands some seven hundred years earlier, but for many years was considered of value only for its supposed curative properties. By the 1500's, however, its use had taken on a decidedly pietistic coloration and called for an elaborate ritual, the *cha-no-yu*, or "tea ceremony," which required its own detached or semidetached shrine, the "House of Peace," constructed according to precise specifications and designed to provide the serenity requisite to meaningful contemplation and spiritual rapport.

The rite was—and remains—an incredibly elaborate affair involving an attention to protocol, etiquette, dress, symbolism, and self-abnegation calibrated to an almost agonizing nicety. As *The Book of Tea*, the classic manual, instructs the novitiate, "The order of precedence having been mutually agreed upon . . . the guests [who already have demonstrated their humility by bending low and creeping into the room through a small door] one by one will enter noiselessly and take their seats, first making obeisance to the picture or flower arrangement on the *tokonoma*. The host will not enter the room until all the guests have seated themselves and quiet reigns with nothing to break the silence save the note of the boiling water in the iron kettle. . . ."

Not every Occidental's cup of Tetley, to be sure, and a far, far cry from the hot water, served in a knockabout china cup with a teabag on the side and crashed onto a formica tabletop by the waitress at the local diner.

9

A Beginning or an End?

Why, you might just as well say that "I see what I eat" is the same thing as "I eat what I see."

Lewis Carroll
Alice's Adventures in Wonderland

INTERNATIONAL GASTRONOMY has undergone startling changes in the three decades since World War II. Accessible jet travel has familiarized millions of people of moderate means with alien foods, cultures, and customs, breaking down age-old taboos and prejudices in the process and creating a new social phenomenon, the middle-class epicure.

In Japan, where meat-eaters were despised for centuries, as much for their odor as their flouting of Buddhist strictures, businessmen now attack beefsteaks with the avidity of Texans—and pay the price of truffled *foie gras* for the privilege; Americans who once regarded raw fish with a squeamishness bordering on sheer terror today down *sashimi* with the equanimity of pelicans; the Englishman on the Riviera sips *pastis* with a knowing air, while the Frenchman at the next table casually knocks back a whisky-and-soda; travelers to Italy have become connoisseurs of the cream, butter, and rice cookery of the north after decades of believing that meatballs, spaghetti, and tomato sauce were the be-all and end-all of Italian food; Germans in Barcelona find in *caldo Gallego* that the more things change, the more they remain the same. Even the once-inevitable Vienna sausages, cheddar cheese dips, and potato chips of the American cocktail party, now thoroughly infra dig, have been replaced by *yakitori, bourrek,* and *quiche* as "gourmet cooking" becomes a shibboleth of an era that has yet to put its first gourmet into a pot.

If haute cuisine can be said to survive anywhere today, it survives in its birthplace, France. Revitalized by a host of younger chefs, men whose shared passions are for simplification and experimentation, the art of eating well brings pleasure to a new generation of gastronomes, both amateur and professional.

Thus far at least, Americans have been the chief beneficiaries of all this gastronomic acculturation, although not every American might see it that way. Those of relatively recent vintage, for example, who have maintained close ties with their ethnic heritages, might take an understandably dim view of a situation in which a sudden demand for hitherto esoteric items (brains, sweetbreads, kidneys, marrow bones, mussels, squid, artichokes, and zucchini, to name a few), long the inexpensive staples of their traditional cuisines, has elevated them to the status of delicacies, causing their prices to rise accordingly. And then there's the American black, who can only look on bemused by the current popularity of the soul food he ate for generations because that was all he could get.

The postwar impact of American gastronomy (if that's the word) abroad hasn't been an unmixed blessing either. When the hot dog and *hamburguesa* become ubiquitous features of the Spanish cityscape, supermarkets (to say nothing of the Kellogg's cornflakes on their shelves) appear in Paris, Blimpie Base sandwich shops sprout in London, and Mt. Fuji can almost be glimpsed through the golden arches of McDonald's, a concern for the global future of the art of eating well isn't necessarily a manifestation of paranoia. And while the good citizens of Périgord aren't likely to start drenching their truffles in ketchup in the foreseeable future, the southern French chef to add Jell-O and marshmallows to his vaunted *salade niçoise,* or Parisian restaurateurs to serve peanut-butter omelets, the quieter, more pervasive effects of Americanization on international cookery aren't altogether reassuring.

At home, Americans today are concerned with gastronomy to an unprecedented degree, but they haven't begun to learn the fundamentals of sound culinary practice, the building blocks whose uses are hardly the concomitants of instant expertise and without which a cuisine worth the name cannot develop. Cookbooks of every conceivable description clog shelves across the nation, the once-trusty can opener has been replaced by all manner of arcane utensils, "organic" food outlets and esoterically stocked specialty shops proliferate like fruit flies, cookery instructors achieve TV stardom, lifelong beer drinkers murmur sagely of the "nose" of a particular Chassagne-Montrachet, and *paella* becomes as familiar in Providence as in Valencia. Rugula is the "in" salad green (or was at this writing), suburban matrons make *pesto* with basil grown in windowboxes, shrimp cocktail gives way to *prosciutto* and melon as the chic appetizer, and Mom's apple pie, like the republic for which it stands, becomes an object of derision.

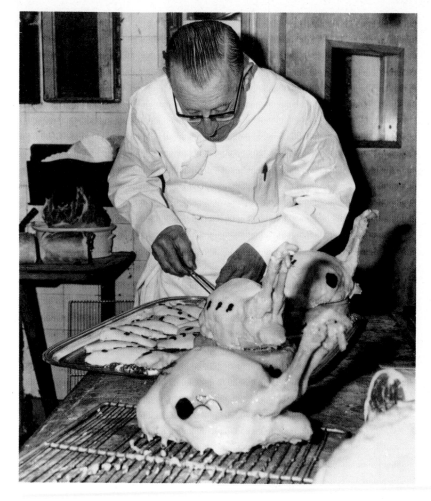

A special artistry distinguishes the master chef, setting him apart from talents of lesser rank. The dishes he produces please the eye as well as the palate, and this process of "finishing" requires skills developed through years of specialized training. At right, a chef at Maxim's, a Parisian temple of haute cuisine, applies aspic glaze to fowl previously decorated with truffles. At lower left, a Chinese chef puts the finishing touches on a banquet centerpiece carved entirely from fresh turnips.

And still Americans remain abysmally ignorant of the basic nature of their foods. We still tend to conceive of and plan for one dish and one meal at a time, buying not meats and vegetables, but packages, and paying for parts what the whole would cost if we had the sense to realize that we could still impress guests with, say, *suprêmes de volaille Rossini* if we bought a whole chicken, detached the breast ourselves—a ludicrously simple operation—and used the remainder of the bird to make a couple of additional main dishes, a good soup, and the basis for a sauce or two.

A French or Chinese cook seemingly can extract more from a duck than was there to begin with, making something eminently edible out of everything but the feathers and the bird's quack (the webbing of ducks' feet, for example, discarded before the bird reaches the American consumer, is considered a delicacy in China). In this country probably no more than 30 per cent of the fowl is consumed and the rest—a marvelous source of pâtés, conserves, soups, stocks, and cooking fat—is junked. As with the duck, so with the lobster, which, although good for at least three splendid dishes, is picked at only for its few mouthfuls of tail and claw meat, with its sweet body flesh, useful shell, coral, and tomalley usually consigned to the garbage can. The shrimp and rock lobster, subject to even worse indignities, are deprived of everything but their tails before reaching the market—an affront to civilized living hardly less heinous than cutting off Gainsborough's *Blue Boy* from the waist up and one that robs the consumer (who in any case covers the cost of the truncation) of a superb source of sauces and bisques. And as with these crustaceans, so with many of the root vegetables we buy, which reach the market bereft of green tops that in many cases would have made tasty and nutritious additions to salads and soups.

To return to the chicken for a moment, what we buy at the local shopping center isn't so much a fowl as a technological Frankenstein's monster; an androgynous, factory-produced, artificially fattened basket case that never saw daylight or scratched dirt, displays the symptoms of a chemically induced jaundice, and is packaged to resemble not a mortal bird that lived, suffered, and died in the manner of all earth's creatures, but only the neighboring package. Its feet, potentially the valuable components of a soup, are gone, and the absence of most of the skin of its neck, which one's grandmother might have stuffed with a savory mixture of odds and ends, probably heralds the imminent disappearance of the neck itself. It has had the identical lifespan—seven weeks to the day (if not the hour)—as its fellows and contains no dark meat by any reasonable definition of the term. Its net weight deviates from that of its neatly wrapped neighbors by no more than a couple of ounces and its flavor is virtually nil. Nowhere in current American gastronomy is allowance made for the stringy old cock that, having begat generations of its kind and finally been consigned to the pot, required prolonged cooking but lent character and distinction to a soup or stew.

Foodstuffs in this country are no longer what they are but what packaging makes them seem. Fish, flesh, and fowl, beans, spinach, and okra—all come out of the same rectilinear mold. In the name of hygiene we have deprived ourselves of any cheese worth eating, squaring up unsatisfactory substitutes to conform to an abstract ideal. In the name of safety we have reduced a wealth of native mushrooms to one tasteless species, even while pumping our beef and bacon full of possible carcinogens. We have bleached our wheat, refined our rice, deodorized our fish, and made of our soups substances rich in polysyllables intelligible only to chemists but devoid of apprehendable meaning to the 245 sensors on each of our tongues.

While we have given more and more lip service to the value of costly "organic" foods that, for all we know, drip with chemical pesticides, we increasingly deprive the bulk of our foods of any evidence of their organic characteristics, shaping them not for the pot but the shelf, prizing them not for whatever intrinsic goodness they still may have but cosmeticizing them to conform with our peculiar notions of decorum. Even as we pride ourselves on our newly acquired taste for the exotic and our receptivity to new gustatory experiences, we standardize our vegetables and render the creatures we devour increasingly unrecognizable as beings that shared our own animal characteristics and functions. In the process we waste what whole peoples might feed on, and we debase our cuisine by crippling its potential.

The essence of a true cuisine, however costly a few of its components may be, is thrift; the talent for parlaying a few ingredients from dish to dish and meal to meal, investing each along the way with its

Man's compulsion to improve upon nature has altered—but not always greatly improved—virtually every staple item in his diet. Through selective breeding and hybridizing, man has produced beefier cattle, fatter hogs, and high-yield "miracle" grains. But by this same process he has also robbed the capon of its distinctive taste and the tomato of its former succulence. On the whole, however, agronomy and animal husbandry have forced nature to produce an ever-greater bounty over an ever-longer growing season.

maximum potential for nourishment and enjoyment. Any reasonably solvent fool with a can opener and a wine guide at his disposal can regale his guests with Beluga caviar, Strasbourg *foie gras*, and a bottle of vintage champagne. A rich, viscous, aromatic, and impeccably clarified consommé, though, the elegant product of humble leftovers, is an altogether different matter and one that requires understanding and artistry. Until we recognize this in principle, not all the knowledgeability in the world will convert dilettantism into gastronomy, for gastronomy is, after all, an art, and art is no easy taskmaster.

Of course, gastronomy and cookery aren't interchangeable terms, and just as the concertgoer isn't obliged to know the mechanics of music to appreciate what he hears, the gourmet needn't be a cook to enjoy what he eats. But just as the music lover is dependent for his satisfaction on the performer and a score, the gastronome is dependent on the cook and a cuisine. If that cook is deprived of decent ingredients he can no more perform than could a cellist without his bow.

To further deprive the cook of a cuisine—a recognizable style of cooking based on continuity and sound principles—is little different from depriving the conductor of both his score and musical background. This, unfortunately and with relatively few exceptions, is the prevailing condition in America, where a host of adverse factors militate against the production of foods that look, taste, feel, or smell as they should, where useful parts of foods either never reach the consumer or are discarded when they do, where "experts" assure us that the use of bouillon cubes, packaged mixes, canned soups, and the like will make instant gourmet cooks of us all, and where we are conditioned from infancy to the consumption of expensive, sugared junk. Until today's burgeoning interest in cookery evolves from a fad into a genuine commitment spurred not by the need to impress but to do an honest workmanlike job in an honest workmanlike manner, gastronomy in America will be in a rather bad way. And unless we are quick to reverse the situation—an obviously tall order—it will get a lot worse.

In a world half-starved and faced with the alarming prospect of a doubled population just three decades away, an absorption with the art of good eating may seem frivolous at the very least, murderous at worst. As Reay Tannahill has written, "for twelve thousand years there has been a steady undercurrent of antagonism between those whose diet consists mainly of grain and those who depend on animal foods." Such an antagonism isn't likely to cool while a minority of the world's inhabitants fattens itself on grain-fattened beef and the majority goes hungry. Continuing misuse and mistreatment of natural resources is in no way calculated to alleviate the drastic depletion of once-abundant supplies of fish and shellfish in the Mediterranean, the western Atlantic, and elsewhere. An acute worldwide fertilizer shortage bodes no good whatever for soil that in many parts of the globe has been worked and irrigated to the point of exhaustion. Seemingly indestructible strains of crop-destroying pests proliferate happily while their natural predators are decimated by chemical insecticides. The waters that sustain our very lives are themselves dying of the not-very-tender mercies of various pollutants—the grim litany could be expanded almost indefinitely.

With problems of such magnitude facing us, can we in good conscience continue to concern ourselves with the art of eating well? We can and should. Inevitably, adjustments will have to be made. Inevitably, the diets of various cultures—our own included—will have to undergo various changes, some to their impoverishment, some to their enrichment. But if the history of gastronomy has shown us anything, it has demonstrated that cuisines are the products of working intelligently with the materials at hand. If the Italians ate better after the introduction of the tomato, the French when they learned the uses of the potato, and the Szechuanese when the capsicum pepper arrived in China, they hadn't done all that badly without these innovations.

Gastronomy will endure because at its best—and a relative handful of celebrated but inconsequential gluttons notwithstanding—it is an expression of man's capacity for realizing the fullest potential of the resources, however limited they may be, at his command, and of his innate need to order and beautify his existence. It will endure because it is the essential science among man's sciences, the essential art among his arts. It has provided the foundations on which most of his other sciences and much of his technology were built and the sustenance on which his other arts have flourished. Perhaps the late A. J. Liebling summed it up best:

> The Proust *madeleine* phenomenon is now as firmly established in folklore as Newton's apple or Watt's steam engine. The man ate a tea biscuit, the taste evoked memories, he wrote a book. . . . In the light of what Proust wrote with so mild a stimulus, it is the world's loss that he did not have a heartier appetite. On a dozen Gardiner's Island oysters, a bowl of clam chowder, a peck of steamers, some bay scallops, three sautéed soft-shelled crabs, a few ears of fresh-picked corn, a thin swordfish steak of generous area, a pair of lobsters, and a Long Island duck, he might have written a masterpiece.

Overleaf: *Giuseppe Arcimboldo executed this fanciful personification of summer in the sixteenth century.*

PIÈCE DE RÉSISTANCE

In the realm of the culinary arts, New York City is unique among the great cities of the world in its lack of close identification with a national style of cooking. Thus while a visitor to Paris, Rome, or Tokyo selects without hesitation a restaurant featuring native dishes, the same person in New York ponders an array of excellent restaurants featuring the foods of nearly fifty countries. With its characteristic flair, New York has turned this lack of a clearly defined "American" cuisine into a virtue—by providing a showcase for the foods of the diverse national communities that comprise its population. The more than 23,000 restaurants operating in the five boroughs of New York present both visitors and residents alike with a staggering number of gustatory experiences. As an introduction to this gastronome's paradise, Jay Jacobs and the Editors of Newsweek Books have invited the chefs of twenty-six of the finest restaurants in New York to share the recipes for a few of their outstanding dishes. This sampler of the cooking styles of sixteen nations contains imaginative and challenging dishes that attest to the high standards of preparation and service these restaurants have made their trademark. A number of the following recipes call for ingredients available only in specialty shops, but this fact should not discourage the adventurous amateur anxious to re-create these dishes in his own kitchen.

COPENHAGEN

(Danish)
68 West 58th Street

HERRING IN MUSTARD SAUCE

½ cup mayonnaise
⅓ cup sour cream
¼ cup commercially prepared Dijon
  mustard
⅓ cup finely chopped dill weed
4 marinated herring fillets, cut into
  1-inch pieces
Fresh dill sprigs for garnish

Danish Mustard:
½ cup dry mustard
7 tablespoons sugar
¼ cup boiling water
2 teaspoons Worcestershire sauce
½ teaspoon imported Swedish vinegar or cider vinegar
3 tablespoons vegetable oil
¼ teaspoon salt

To make Danish mustard. Combine the mustard and sugar in a bowl. Beat in the boiling water to make a paste. Beat in the remaining ingredients. Refrigerate.

To make mustard sauce. Combine the mayonnaise, sour cream, Dijon mustard and 3½ tablespoons Danish mustard, and chopped dill in a mixing bowl. Stir in herring pieces and chill. Spoon the herring and sauce into a serving dish and garnish with dill sprigs. Serves 8–10.

LIVER PATÉ

1 pound pork liver
1 large onion, chopped
8 anchovies
3 eggs

½ teaspoon salt
¼ teaspoon pepper
4 truffles, chopped (optional)

Grind liver, onion, and anchovies to a fine consistency. Add eggs, salt, pepper, and chopped truffles and mix. Put mixture into an oblong baking dish, set in a slightly larger baking dish filled with water to a depth of ½ inch, and bake for 1 hour at 250°. Cool in baking dish before serving. Serves 6–8.

TENDERLOIN OF PORK

3 pounds pork tenderloin
12 pitted prunes
3 apples, cut into small pieces
½ cup butter

Consommé or water
Flour
Salt and pepper to taste

Remove sinews from loin, cut meat open lengthwise, stuff with fruit, and tie loin together. Brown meat in butter in a deep pot. When golden brown, add enough consommé or water to cover meat and simmer for ½ hour. Remove meat from pot, thicken cooking liquid with a little flour blended in water and pour resultant gravy over meat. Salt and pepper to taste. Serves 6.

ROAST GOOSE

1 12- to 14-pound goose
1 lemon, quartered
1 tablespoon salt
¼ teaspoon pepper

4 cups quartered red apples
4 cups pitted prunes
2 cups boiling water
4 whole red apples

Wash the goose thoroughly. Remove pin feathers and other small feathers. Singe any remaining feathers. Wipe dry. Rub inside and out with the lemon quarters. Combine salt and pepper and rub over inner and outer surfaces of bird. Stuff with alternate spoonfuls of quartered apples and pitted prunes. Truss. Place in a shallow roasting pan and prick surface of goose all over with a sharp fork. Place in a 450° oven for 20 minutes. Reduce heat to 350° and continue roasting for about 3 hours, or 15 minutes per pound. After the first hour, remove bird from the oven and pour off all the accumulated grease. Baste with hot water. Return to the oven and continue roasting, basting with hot water every ½ hour. Prick whole apples well and place in roasting pan during the last 40 minutes of cooking time. Use to garnish serving platter. (If a layer of fat remains under the skin, the blunt edge of a table knife passed over the skin will help to press out the melted fat.) Serves about 10.

(German)
110 East 14th Street

PFIFFERLINGE IN RAHMSAUCE
(Wild Mushrooms in Sour Cream Sauce)

1 medium onion	8 ounces brown sauce
¼ pound bacon	4 ounces sour cream
1 pound wild mushrooms	Fresh dill for garnish

Sauté onions and bacon in a saucepan until golden brown. Add mushrooms. In a separate dish mix brown sauce and sour cream. Combine with mushrooms and simmer for 3–4 minutes. Garnish with fresh dill. Serves 4.

PFIRSICHKALTSCHALE
(Cold Peach Soup)

2 pounds fresh peaches	1 2-inch piece of stick cinnamon
1 quart water	2 teaspoons powdered arrowroot
1 quart red wine	1 cup heavy cream, whipped
1 pound sugar	

Wash fruit, cut in half, and remove pits. Cover fruit with water and wine in an enamel kettle. Add sugar and cinnamon. Cook until fruit is soft. Put through a sieve. Reheat most of fruit mixture, reserving a small amount. Mix arrowroot with reserved mixture when cool, and stir into the rest of the mixture. Bring to a boil for 1–2 minutes. Chill. Serve in a large soup tureen garnished with whipped cream. Serves 6.

LÜCHOW'S HOUSE PLATTER

2–3 cups mashed potatoes	2 pieces knockwurst
2 cups sauerkraut or weinkraut	2 pieces bauernwurst
2 pieces boiled beef	1 long or 2 small pieces bratwurst

All ingredients should be cooked before dish is assembled. Shape mashed potatoes around the wall of a shallow oval casserole. Use a spatula to smooth the surface. Put sauerkraut in center of dish. Place boiled beef in center with knockwurst, bauernwurst, and bratwurst around it. Put under broiler for a few minutes until potatoes turn golden brown. Serves 2 to 4.

SCHWÄRZWALDER KIRSCHTORTE
(Black Forest Cherry Torte)

1 quart large black cherries
½ cup kirsch
5 cups confectioners' sugar
3 tablespoons cornstarch
1 cup butter

3 egg yolks
2 8-inch chocolate sponge cake layers, each one-inch thick
1 cup finely shaved bittersweet
chocolate

Wash cherries, remove stems and pits. Mix kirsch and 1 cup sugar and pour over fruit in a large saucepan. Let stand at least 2 hours, then heat to boiling. Mix cornstarch with 2 tablespoons cherry juice and stir into cherries. Cook and stir until slightly thickened. Remove from heat and allow to cool. (The mixture should have the consistency of thin jelly.) Cream butter and remaining sugar together. Beat egg yolks into this mixture and continue beating until mixture is light and fluffy. Place layer of cake on plate. Make a border around the edge with butter mixture and spread some butter cream in a circle in center of the cake. Spread cooled, thickened cherry mixture between butter-cream border and center. Place second layer on top. Press down sufficiently to make layers stick together. Cover top and sides of both layers with remaining butter cream. Sprinkle top with chocolate. Serves 8.

(Belgian)
115 East 54th Street

EELS AU VERTE

3 pounds small eels, skinned and cut
into 2-inch pieces
Flour for dredging
6 tablespoons butter
2 tablespoons finely chopped shallots
6 tablespoons chopped fresh chervil
2 tablespoons chopped parsley
4 tablespoons chopped sorrel
5 ounces chopped spinach

3 chopped fresh sage leaves (or ¼
teaspoon dried)
1 small sprig fresh tarragon (or ¼
teaspoon dried)
½ bottle dry white wine
Salt and pepper to taste
4 egg yolks, beaten
2 ounces fresh lemon juice

After washing and drying eels, dust them lightly with flour. Heat butter in a heavy skillet and sautè the eels until golden brown. Add the herbs and wine, mix-ing thoroughly, and season to taste with salt and pepper. Cover and simmer gently over low heat for 12 minutes. Carefully remove eels to a bowl. Stir egg yolks into the sauce and beat until the mixture is well blended and thickened. Add lemon juice. Mix well and pour over eels. Chill before serving. Serves 6.

WATERZOÏ DE VOLAILLE À LA GANTOISE
(Chicken Stew)

1 stalk celery, cut into julienne strips
3 leeks (with green tops removed)
2 medium-sized carrots
1 medium-sized onion (quartered)
3 tablespoons butter
2 quarts chicken broth

Bouquet garni: thyme, bay leaf,
parsley, tied in bay leaf
1 4-pound chicken, trussed
¼ pound butter
¾ cup heavy cream
Juice of ½ lemon
3 egg yolks
Parsley for garnish

Place celery, leeks, carrots, and onion quarters in a 5-quart casserole. Add tablespoons of butter. Slowly simmer vegetables in butter for 4–5 minutes. Add chicken broth and herbs and cover casserole. Cook over a low flame for about half an hour, then add the whole chicken. Continue cooking over a low flame for another half hour. Remove the vegetables and chicken from the stock. Bring the stock to a boil and continue cooking until the liquid is reduced by one third. In another pot melt the butter and add the reduced chicken stock, heavy cream, and lemon juice. Beat the mixture with a whisk for 1 minute. Remove from the heat. Add egg yolks and beat rapidly. Strain and pour over the chicken and vegetables. Garnish with chopped parsley and serve immediately, in soup plates, with boiled, peeled potatoes. Serves 4.

FILET DE SOLE OSTENDAISE AU GEVREY CHAMBERTIN

4 medium-sized soles (fillet, reserving the bones)
3 ounces butter
1 medium-sized carrot, split
1 onion, chopped
1 stalk celery, chopped
2 minced shallots
½ pound mushrooms (separate caps and stems)

1 sprig each of thyme, basil, and parsley
3 bay leaves
8 ounces dry white wine
14 ounces Gevrey Chambertin or another fine red wine
5 ounces veal stock
3 ounces anchovy butter (butter mixed with finely chopped anchovy fillet)

Melt butter in a heavy 2-quart casserole. Add carrot, onion, celery, shallots, mushroom stems, thyme, basil, parsley, bay leaves, and sole bones. Cover with white and red wines. Bring to a boil and simmer for 2 hours. Strain broth, pour into casserole, and add veal stock and anchovy butter. Simmer for at least ½ hour to condense further. Fold sole fillets and arrange them in a herringbone pattern on a fireproof platter or copper oval pan. Pour sauce over the fillets and cook approximately 10 to 15 minutes. Garnish with mushrooms caps sautéed in butter. Serve with small boiled potatoes or rice pilaf. Serves 4.

Cafe Argenteuil

(French)
253 East 52nd Street

MOUSSE DE TRUITES NANTAISE

1 1-pound skinned and boned trout
3 egg whites
3 cups heavy cream
½ pound mushrooms
2 tablespoons butter
Dry white wine
Lemon juice
Salt and pepper to taste

Sauce Nantaise:
1 cup dry white wine
½ cup chopped shallots
1 bay leaf
2 ounces heavy cream
8–12 tablespoons butter
Salt and pepper to taste

Pass trout through a meat grinder 3 or 4 times until it is very finely ground. Add egg whites, one at a time, mixing well with wooden spoon. Cool the mixture in the refrigerator for at least 1 hour. Slowly add 3 cups of heavy cream. Chop the mushrooms very finely and sauté them in butter. When they are soft, add a little white wine, lemon juice, salt and pepper to taste, and cook until done. When mushrooms are cold, blend them into the fish mixture. Pour into a buttered ring mold, place in a slightly larger pan ⅔ full of water, and bake in a 400° oven for about 30 minutes. Test for doneness by placing a toothpick in the mousse; it should be hot upon removal. Unmold and serve with Sauce Nantaise. Serves 4.

To make Sauce Nantaise: Place white wine, shallots, and bay leaf in saucepan. Reduce until almost dry. Add the heavy cream and reduce a little. Off heat, beat in 2 teaspoons of the butter until just melted. Over low heat, beat in remaining butter (more for a thicker sauce, less for a thinner sauce), season, and press through a sieve.

CREAM OF MUSSEL SOUP MAXIME

2 pounds mussels, scrubbed and debearded
¼ pound butter
1¼ cups dry white wine
½ cup finely chopped shallots
½ cup finely chopped onion
Salt and pepper to taste
2 cups chopped leeks
1 stalk celery, diced
1 quart consommé or water
2 large potatoes, peeled and diced
⅝ cup heavy cream

Put 6 tablespoons of butter, mussels, wine, shallots, onions, salt and pepper in a fireproof dish, cover, bring to a boil, reduce heat and simmer 25 minutes. In a separate casserole combine remaining butter, leeks, celery, consommé or water and cook about 1 hour. Add the potatoes and salt and pepper. Continue cooking 25 minutes more. Put this mixture through a foodmill. Return to casserole and set aside. Remove mussels from shells and put them through foodmill. Add this puree to potato mixture. Strain mussel broth and add to soup along with the cream. Bring to a boil over low heat, add more butter, and season to taste. Strain entire mixture, extracting all juices. Serve at once. Serves 6–8.

GRENADINS DE VEAU AU CHABLIS

4 boneless veal cutlets
Flour for dredging
2 tablespoons butter
4 medium-sized fresh mushrooms, sliced
1 ounce Chablis or other dry white wine
2 shallots, minced
3 ounces veal stock
Salt and pepper to taste

Season the cutlets, dip them in flour, and sauté them in the butter for about 2 minutes on each side. Do not overcook or the veal will become dry. Remove from heat, keep warm. Add the mushrooms to pan juices, brown lightly. Add the wine and the shallots and reduce almost completely. Add the veal stock and salt and pepper to taste. Heat and pour over veal. Serves 2.

FRUIT TART

1 9-inch unbaked pie or tart shell
4 egg yolks
1 cup sugar
¼ cup plus 1 tablespoon flour
1 tablespoon vanilla
1 pint milk, boiling
Fresh peaches, skinned, pitted, and halved
¼ cup apricot preserves, diluted with two tablespoons Cointreau

Beat egg yolks and sugar until lemon colored, stir in flour. Add vanilla to milk and stir into egg mixture. Cook mixture in double boiler, beating slowly until small bubbles appear and the cream thickens. Pour into shell. Cover top with the fruit and bake in 350° oven for about 1 hour or until fruit is done. Brush with apricot mixture. Serves 4–6.

JEAN VERGNES'S SEAFOOD CRÊPES

(French)
58 East 65th Street

Crêpes with Fines Herbes:
1½ cups sifted flour
2 eggs
¼ teaspoon salt
2½ cups milk
1 tablespoon each chopped fresh tarragon, parsley, and chives
3 tablespoons melted butter
Filling:
3 tablespoons butter
2 tablespoons finely chopped shallots
⅓ cup dry white wine
1 tablespoon each finely chopped chives, parsley, and tarragon
1 cup lump crab meat
1 cup finely diced lobster meat
1 cup finely diced shrimp
Salt and pepper to taste
Melted butter for brushing crêpes

Curry Sauce:
4½ tablespoons butter
1 clove garlic
⅓ cup finely chopped onion
⅓ cup finely chopped celery
3 tablespoons chopped carrot
2 tablespoons flour
2 tablespoons curry powder
½ bay leaf
2 sprigs parsley
2 sprigs fresh thyme (or ½ teaspoon dried)
1¾ cups chicken broth
Salt and pepper to taste
Sauce Piquante:
2 tablespoons Dijon or Düsseldorf mustard
4 tablespoons bottled Sauce Diable*
3 tablespoons bottled Sauce Robert*
¼ teaspoon Tabasco sauce
¼ teaspoon Worcestershire sauce
1¼ cups heavy cream
Salt and pepper to taste

To make crêpes with fines herbes. Combine the flour, eggs, and salt in a mixing bowl. Gradually add the milk, stirring constantly with a wire whisk. Strain the batter into a mixing bowl, then add the herbs and melted butter. Heat a six- to seven-inch seasoned crêpe pan and brush it lightly with butter. Ladle a little of the batter in, swirling the pan around until the bottom is thoroughly covered. Cook until lightly browned on one side. Flip and cook briefly on the second side. Repeat the procedure until the batter is used up. Yields 16–20 crêpes.

To make curry sauce. Heat three tablespoons of butter in a saucepan and add the garlic, onion, celery, and carrot. Cook, stirring, until onion is wilted. Add the flour and cook, stirring, about 3 minutes. Stir in the curry powder, bay leaf, parsley and thyme. Using a wire whisk, continue to stir briskly while adding the broth. Simmer, covered, stirring occasionally, about 30 minutes. Put the mixture, including soft vegetables, through a fine sieve, using a wooden spoon. Swirl in the remaining butter and add salt and pepper to taste.

To make sauce piquante. In a saucepan combine all the ingredients. Simmer, stirring occasionally, about 10 minutes.

To make filling. Place the three tablespoons of butter in a saucepan and add the shallots. Cook briefly, stirring, and add the wine. Reduce liquid by half. Add the herbs and seafood and stir to blend. Sprinkle with salt and pepper to taste and cook briefly, stirring, until heated through.

159

Preheat the oven to 250°. Slowly heat sauces. Spoon equal portions of filling into the center of each crêpe, roll crêpes, and place them in a shallow, ovenproof casserole. Butter a sheet of wax paper and place it, buttered side down, over the crêpes. Cover and set in the oven. Bake briefly, until just heated through but not piping hot. Serve on hot plates, spooning a little curry sauce on half of each crêpe, a little sauce piquante on the other half. Serves 8–10.

*These sauces are available in many supermarkets and in most fine food outlets.

La Petite Marmite

(French)
5 Mitchell Place

LES MOULES À LA MOUTARDE
(Mussels in Mustard Mayonnaise)

4 pounds mussels
Salt and pepper to taste
1 small onion

6–8 ounces dry white wine
Mayonnaise
Dijon mustard

Clean and debeard the mussels thoroughly. Place them in a casserole with salt, pepper, onion, and white wine. Bring to a boil and cook for about 5 minutes. Remove from heat. Remove mussels from shells and place in a mixing bowl. Once cool, mix them with sufficient mayonnaise, lightly flavored with mustard, to cover. Serves 4.

LA PETITE MARMITE

4 pounds lean beef
2 pounds chicken, cut in pieces
1 marrow bone
Bouquet garni

2 carrots
2 leeks
2 turnips
1 celery heart

Place the beef, chicken, marrow bone, and bouquet garni in a casserole. Add sufficient water to cover the ingredients. Bring to a boil and cook for 20 minutes, skimming grease off top of liquid. Add carrots, leeks, turnips, and celery, all wrapped in cheesecloth. Cook for 15 minutes and remove vegetables. Continue to cook chicken for another 15 minutes and remove, leaving beef to cook another hour. Cut the beef and chicken into small portions. Skim the broth again and then pour it through a sieve. Serve with meat, chicken, and vegetables. Serves 4.

LES ASPERGES VINAIGRETTE

32 jumbo asparagus
Pinch of salt
2 pinches freshly ground pepper

1 tablespoon wine vinegar
1 tablespoon mustard
2 tablespoons vegetable oil

Peel the stalks and trim the woody ends of the asparagus. Tie the asparagus in bunches of 10 to 12 with kitchen string, and steam upright in an asparagus steamer (or in a large kettle, boil in salted water to cover) for 8–10 minutes or until tender. Remove the asparagus, drain on paper towels, and remove string. Dry and allow to cool. Prepare vinaigrette by combining the salt, pepper, wine vinegar, mustard, and vegetable oil. Pour over asparagus before serving. Serves 4.

LE PONT NEUF

(French)
212 East 53rd Street

CRAB FINGERS DIJONNAISE

24 fresh or frozen crab claw sections
Flour for dredging
1 cup milk
1 egg yolk
½ teaspoon salt
¼ teaspoon pepper
1 cup bread crumbs

1 cup clarified butter
1 cup velouté sauce
1 teaspoon Dijon mustard
½ cup heavy cream
½ ounce cognac
1 teaspoon chopped parsley

Dredge crab claws in flour. Beat together milk, egg yolk, salt and pepper. Dip crab claws into mixture and dredge in bread crumbs. Coat well. Sauté crab claws in clarified butter until browned; then set them aside and prepare sauce. Mix a cup of velouté sauce with Dijon mustard. Place in a saucepan and, over moderate heat, add heavy cream and cognac. Simmer for 10 minutes. Strain and serve over crab claws. Garnish with parsley. Serves 6.

CAPON BREASTS PONT NEUF

2 capon breasts (about 3 pounds)
1 teaspoon salt
½ teaspoon pepper
1 cup milk
1 cup flour
2 ounces clarified butter
1 teaspoon chopped shallots
½ cup boiled chestnuts

1 tablespoon chopped truffles (optional)
½ ounce cognac
1 ounce white wine
1 cup heavy cream
2 ounces veal stock or consommé
1 egg yolk
1 cup Bordelaise sauce
2 cups sautéed mushrooms

Bone and skin the capon breasts and slice them into finger-sized pieces. Season these with salt and pepper, dip in milk and then in flour. Brown them in hot clarified butter, keeping the slices separated. Add chopped shallots, chestnuts, and truffles. Flame with cognac. Deglaze by adding white wine. Add half the heavy cream and reduce liquid by half. Add veal stock or consommé. Cook over low heat for about 3 minutes. Remove capon and chestnuts to a serving dish. Off heat, beat one egg yolk into sauce. Whip the remaining heavy cream and blend into sauce. Season to taste with salt and pepper and pour over capon pieces. Carefully brown under broiler. Prepare 1 cup of Bordelaise sauce. Serve capons with sautéed mushrooms and Bordelaise sauce. Serves 4.

MOUSSE AUX FRAISES
(Strawberry Mousse)

2 quarts fresh strawberries
Water to cover
½ pound plus 4 tablespoons sugar
1 package unflavored gelatin
¼ cup hot water

1 pint heavy cream
5 eggs, separated
1 ounce kirsch
Strawberry halves for garnish

Prepare fruit syrup by cooking strawberries in water to cover and ½ pound sugar until the liquid reaches 230° on a candy thermometer. Strain through a medium sieve. Soften gelatin in hot water and add to syrup. Whip heavy cream, gradually adding 2 tablespoons of sugar, and refrigerate. Beat egg whites until they form soft peaks, add remaining sugar gradually, and beat until mixture forms stiff peaks. Refrigerate. In largest bowl of an electric mixer, beat egg yolks until they foam, add fruit syrup, and beat 5 more minutes. Add kirsch. Reduce speed to lowest cycle and add beaten egg whites and heavy cream. Pour into serving dish and refrigerate. Serve decorated with strawberry halves.

Lutèce

(French)
249 East 50th Street

MOUSSE DE PIGEON AU GENIÈVRE

¾ pound pigeon, with bones (or 1 small squab)
½ pound chicken livers
Salt and pepper to taste

1 cup duck fat, reserved from roasting 2 5-pound ducks, or 1 cup lard
6 blue juniper berries
6 tablespoons dry white wine

Preheat oven to 250°. Put the pigeon, bones included, and the chicken livers through the fine opening of a meat grinder. Add salt and pepper to the mixture, one-third of the fat, and the juniper berries. Mix the resultant "dough" until smooth with a wooden spoon or by hand. Put the mixture in a saucepan. Set the saucepan in a pan of shallow water on the middle level of the oven. Cook for about 30 minutes. Add the wine, blending well, and cook for another 15 minutes. Push the resultant cooked mousse through a fine sieve and let it cool. Heat the remaining fat until soft and blend with mousse. Pack the mousse in an earthenware dish and refrigerate thoroughly. (For storage purposes, it is desirable to smear the top of the mousse with a thin layer of softened lard.) Serve with toast points. Serves 9.

COQ AU RIESLING

1 3-pound chicken
Salt and pepper
6 tablespoons butter
3 medium-sized shallots

6 ounces cognac
5 ounces sliced mushrooms
9 ounces Riesling wine
3 ounces heavy cream

Clean chicken and cut into quarters. Season with salt and pepper. Melt butter in a skillet and add chicken. Cook over a low fire for 5 minutes. Add shallots and cognac, wait a moment, and set cognac aflame. Add the mushrooms and then the wine. Simmer gently for 30 to 40 minutes. Remove the chicken pieces and arrange them in a casserole. Reduce the sauce, thicken it with heavy cream, and pour over the chicken. Adjust seasonings and serve with hot noodles. Serves 5.

KIRSCH SOUFFLÉ

7 tablespoons butter
¾ cup flour
2 cups milk
6 tablespoons sugar
1 vanilla bean

6 egg yolks
3 ounces kirsch
8 egg whites
Confectioners' sugar

TORTELLINI ALLA PANNA E PROSCIUTTO
(*Tortellini with Cream and Prosciutto*)

50–60 pieces of tortellini*
2 ounces butter
4 tablespoons unsweetened whipped cream

4 thin slices of prosciutto, cut into julienne strips
4 tablespoons Parmesan cheese
Pepper

Boil and drain tortellini. Place them in a pan over a low flame and add butter. Stir until butter melts. Add whipped cream and prosciutto. When cream is boiling add Parmesan and pepper to taste. Mix and serve immediately. Serves 2.

*Prepared tortellini may be purchased at markets featuring Italian foodstuffs.

Aperitivo

(Italian)
29 West 56th Street

POTATO GNOCCHI WITH MUSHROOM SAUCE

2 pounds potatoes
3 tablespoons butter
1 egg
1 pound flour
5 quarts boiling salted water
¼ pound Parmesan cheese
Salt and pepper

Mushroom Sauce:
1 cup chopped onion
1 stalk of celery, chopped
2 tablespoons chopped carrot
½ cup olive oil
½ cup butter
1 cup tomato puree diluted with 1 cup of warm water
½ pound mushrooms, cleaned and sliced
1 tablespoon chopped parsley
Salt and pepper

Boil potatoes in their jackets. When they are cooked, peel and put through a sieve. Add butter, egg, and flour; mix until firm. Roll dough into ¼-inch-thick ropes. Cut into ¾-inch-long pieces. If dough seems soft, sprinkle with more flour. Turn each piece with a fork to dry. Boil 5 quarts of salted water. Drop gnocchi into boiling water and cook until they come to the surface. Drain. Pour into serving dish and add hot mushroom sauce. Sprinkle with Parmesan cheese before serving. Serves 4.

To make mushroom sauce. Sauté onion, celery, and carrot in olive oil and butter until onion is golden. Add tomato paste mixture and simmer uncovered for 25 minutes. Add mushrooms and parsley. Simmer for 10 more minutes. Season to taste with salt and pepper. Serves 4.

CHICKEN APERITIVO

1 2½-pound chicken, cut in pieces
5 tablespoons olive oil
1 small onion, finely chopped
2 shallots, minced
2 sprigs of chives
4 slices of prosciutto, chopped
5 mushrooms, finely chopped

2 bay leaves
1 pinch thyme
2 teaspoons minced parsley
Salt and pepper to taste
1 cup dry white wine
1 cup consommé

In a frying pan heat olive oil. Sauté chicken until golden brown on all sides. Remove from heat and set the chicken aside. Sauté the onion, shallots, and chives. Add the prosciutto, mushrooms, bay leaves, thyme, parsley, and salt and pepper. Cook for about 5 minutes. Add chicken and wine. Cook uncovered for 3 more minutes. Add consommé, and simmer, covered, until chicken is cooked. Serves 4.

ANGIOLINA BUGIE
(*Fried Dough*)

1 pound flour	1 cup sugar
6 eggs	2 tablespoons baking powder
Grated rind of 2 lemons	¼ pound melted butter
4 ounces Marsala	Fat for deep-frying

Sift flour and combine with eggs, lemon rind, Marsala, sugar, baking powder, and melted butter. Mix until dough is very firm. Roll out dough on a very thin cookie sheet and cut into rectangular shapes 4 inches in length. Deep fry in very hot fat until golden. Drain well on absorbent paper. Dust with confectioners' sugar.

Siambelli

50th

(Italian)
46 East 50th Street

SCAMPI RAIMONDO

16 baby Danish lobster tails, shelled and cleaned	*Sauce Raimondo*:
Flour for dredging	1 shallot, finely chopped
½ cup oil	1 clove garlic, finely chopped
½ cup butter	2 tablespoons butter
½ cup dry white wine	2 anchovies, finely chopped
Juice of 1 lemon	5 capers, minced
Salt and pepper to taste	1 tablespoon chopped parsley
8 thin slices of proscuitto or sliced boiled ham, cut in half lengthwise to make 16 slices	½ cup dry white wine
	Few drops lemon juice
16 thin slices mozzarella cheese	½ cup brown sauce
½ cup grated Parmesan cheese	Salt and pepper to taste

Pour oil in a 10-inch skillet and heat over a low flame. Dredge each lobster tail in flour, place in skillet, and cook until golden brown. Drain oil from skillet, add butter and allow it to melt. Add white wine, lemon juice, salt and pepper to taste. Sauté lobster tails in sauce for two minutes, carefully stirring the seafood to avoid burning. Remove the lobster tails from the pan and roll a slice of ham around each one. Set in a baking dish, forming two rows. Place a slice of mozzarella cheese over each rolled lobster tail, sprinkle with grated Parmesan cheese, and bake in a warm oven until cheese is golden brown. Serve with Sauce Raimondo. Serves 8.

To make Sauce Raimondo. Melt butter in a 10-inch skillet and sauté shallot and garlic until golden brown. Add anchovies, capers, and parsley. Simmer 5 minutes. Add wine and lemon juice, mixing well. Stir in brown sauce, season with salt and pepper to taste. Yields 1 cup of sauce.

RUGOLA SALAD

2 bunches rugola
¼ cup olive oil

4 tablespoons vinegar
Salt and pepper

Wash and clean rugola well. Cut off roots just before serving to retain freshness. In a bowl, mix vinegar and salt and pepper. Add olive oil, stir again. Taste to check seasoning and pour over rugola. Toss gently and serve. Serves 4.

RISOTTO MILANESE

1 cup Italian short-grain rice
½ cup butter
½ medium-sized onion, finely
chopped
1 packet saffron powder (softened in
chicken stock)

2 quarts chicken stock (keep hot on a
low flame to use as needed)
¼ pound grated Parmesan cheese
Salt and pepper

Place half of the butter in a heavy casserole and add onion and a pinch of pepper. When the onion is translucent, add rice and a little salt. Stirring rice and butter over a high heat, add the saffron and then a pint and a half of the chicken stock. As the rice thickens add remaining stock. The rice should cook for 20 minutes. When the rice is cooked, lower the heat and add the remaining butter and a handful of the grated parmesan cheese. Mix well and remove from heat. Let rice stand for a minute to settle and then serve, placing the remaining Parmesan cheese in a separate dish. Serves 4.

Romeo Salta

(Italian)
30 West 56th Street

WHITE BEANS AND CAVIAR

2 cups dried white beans
Water to cover
2 teaspoons salt
¼ cup olive oil

¼ teaspoon pepper
½ cup black caviar
Lemon wedges

Wash the beans, cover with water and bring to a boil. Remove from heat and allow beans to soak in water for 1 hour. Drain, add fresh water to cover and bring to a boil. Cover and cook over low heat for 2 hours or until tender, adding the salt after the first hour. Drain and cool. Toss the beans with oil and pepper. Add the caviar, mixing gently. Serve with lemon wedges. Serves 6–8.

PAGLIA E FIENO PAPALINA
(Straw and Hay Pasta)

Egg pasta
Green pasta
1 pound fresh mushrooms
4–6 tablespoons butter
1 clove garlic

½ pound prosciutto, minced
1 cup light cream
½ cup grated Parmesan cheese
Salt to taste

Prepare plain pasta and green pasta doughs according to any standard recipe. Roll them out thinly, leave them to dry for 30 minutes, and then cut into tagliatelle or tagliolini (thick or thin noodles). Leave them to dry on a cloth. Clean and slice the mushrooms. Heat half of the butter in a deep frying pan, add the garlic clove, and sauté gently until browned. Discard the garlic and add the mushrooms. Sprinkle lightly with salt and sauté for 10 minutes. In another pan, melt the remaining butter and fry the prosciutto until browned. Heat the cream in a double boiler. While keeping all these ingredients hot, bring two large pans of salted water to a boil and cook pastas separately. When the noodles are tender but still firm, drain them, turn into a deep, heated serving dish, and toss them together. Dress them with the mushrooms, prosciutto, cream, and grated cheese and serve immediately. Serves 6.

(Spanish)
251 East 53rd Street

ENSALADA ESPANOLA
(Spanish Salad)

1 head of Boston lettuce
½ green pepper, cut in thin strips
8 white asparagus spears, cut into
  1-inch pieces
8 ounces artichoke hearts

1 tomato, cut in quarters
16 Spanish green olives
Salt and pepper to taste
Vinegar and olive oil

Tear lettuce into small pieces and place in a bowl. Add remaining ingredients (oil and vinegar in a ratio of 3:1) and mix with a wooden fork and spoon. Serves 4.

SOPA CASTILLA LA VIEJA
(Almond Soup)

1 cup almonds, sliced
2 tablespoons melted butter
6 cups beef consommé

1 ounce cognac
16 thin slices of bread
Salt to taste

Place almonds in a skillet and heat until golden brown. Add butter and wait until the almonds absorb it. Pour boiling consommé over almonds, bring to a second boil, add cognac, and simmer for 5–10 minutes. Place 4 slices of bread into each of 4 serving bowls, pour soup over them, and serve. Serves 4.

PERDIZ ESTOFADA
(Stewed Partridge)

4 partridges
4 tablespoons olive oil
¼ cup water
2 carrots
1 leek
1 onion
1 bay leaf
1 sprig thyme

Salt to taste
White pepper
2 to 4 whole cloves
2 tablespoons flour
4 tablespoons tomato, finely chopped
¼ cup wine vinegar
Assorted vegetables of your choice
  for garnishing

Wash partridges thoroughly and dry. With a string, tie wings and legs to body. Heat the olive oil in a skillet and fry the partridges until brown. Stop the cooking suddenly by pouring in the water. Add carrots, leek, and onion. Add bay leaf, thyme, salt, white pepper, and cloves. Cover and let cook for some 30–40 minutes. When the partridges are cooked, strain the sauce through a sieve into a pan, thicken with flour and tomato, add vinegar, and finish cooking the sauce. Place the partridges, split in two, on a tray or oval dish, cover with the sauce, and garnish with steamed potatoes, asparagus tips, mushrooms, or green peas, according to taste. Season. Serves 4.

LOBSTER A LA CATALANA

4 6-ounce lobster tails	Salt and pepper
1/3 cup vinegar	1 sprig parsley, chopped
1 cup Spanish olive oil	½ hard-boiled egg, chopped well
2 cloves garlic, chopped	8 green olives, pitted
4 anchovy fillets	8 pimiento strips

Boil lobster tails, let them cool and remove meat from shells. Cut the lobster into slices and place on a plate. Put remaining ingredients in a bowl and mix well. Pour over lobster and serve garnished with pimiento strips. Serves 4.

NATILLAS A LA ESPANOLA
(Spanish Cream Custard)

4 cups of milk	5 tablespoons sugar
1 stick cinnamon	8 ladyfingers
½ teaspoon lemon peel	Crème de cacao
5 egg yolks	

Boil milk with cinnamon and lemon peel, and let it cool. Place egg yolks and sugar in a bowl, blend well, add milk, and pour mixture into the top of a double boiler. When thickened, strain into dessert bowls, let cool, and garnish each serving with two ladyfingers and a small amount of crème de cacao. Serves 4.

Sea-Fare
of the Aegean

(Greek)
25 West 56th Street

RED SNAPPER ANDROS WITH AVGOLEMONO SAUCE

2 pounds filet of red snapper	4 tablespoons flour
1 quart cold water	3 egg yolks
1 pint chicken broth	2 tablespoons fresh lemon juice
½ cup diced carrots	1 teaspoon Maggi sauce
1 small stalk celery, sliced thin	½ cup fresh green peas
1 small onion, diced	Salt to taste
½ cup butter	

Cut red snapper into 4 portions. Place in a skillet and add water, chicken broth, carrots, celery, and onion. Salt to taste. Heat until broth begins to boil, then lower flame and simmer until fish is fork-tender but not cooked through. Remove fish to an ovenproof baking dish and keep warm. Reserve cooked vegetables and liquid. Prepare avgolemono sauce by melting butter in another skillet. Add flour and stir lightly. Add reserved fish broth and stir until thickened and creamy. Beat egg yolks and lemon juice and add to the sauce. Add Maggi sauce, peas, and the cooked carrots, celery, and onion. Pour sauce over red snapper and cook over low flame for 5 minutes. Serves 4.

GREEK SALAD

1 small head Boston lettuce
1 small head Romaine lettuce
3 tomatoes, quartered
2 green peppers, sliced
Greek feta cheese, cut in small pieces
1 cucumber, sliced
Pinch of dried oregano
Shreds of dill
Salt and pepper
½ cup olive oil
2 tablespoons wine vinegar
4 anchovy fillets
1 radish, sliced
8 Greek olives

Tear lettuce into bite-sized pieces and toss with remaining ingredients. Garnish with anchovies, radish, and olives. Serves 4–6.

SHRIMP SANTORINI

24 jumbo shrimp
2 tablespoons flour
½ cup butter
2 fresh tomatoes
Oregano to taste
Grated Parmesan cheese
4 slices Greek feta cheese
Santorini Sauce:
½ cup butter
½ cup minced onions
1 teaspoon minced garlic
1 tablespoon chopped fresh dill
1 tablespoon chopped fresh parsley
¼ teaspoon dried oregano
¼ teaspoon dried basil
2 bay leaves
1 teaspoon sugar
1 #2½ can stewed tomatoes
1 cup ketchup
1 quart chicken broth
1¼ pound live lobster
1½ quarts water
½ cup sherry
1 teaspoon Maggi sauce
Salt and pepper to taste

Peel, devein, and wash shrimps. Dust lightly with flour. Melt butter in a shallow skillet over medium flame, add the shrimps and sauté until golden in color. Place 6 shrimps each in 4 shallow casserole dishes. Cut fresh tomatoes in half and sprinkle tops with oregano and Parmesan cheese. Grill until partly cooked. Place seasoned, grilled tomato halves on top of shrimps in each casseorle. Then place 1 slice of feta cheese on top of each tomato half. Cover with Santorini sauce and bake in 400° oven for 5 minutes. Serves 4.

To make Santorini Sauce. Preheat oven to 350°. Melt butter in a shallow baking pan and add the next 8 ingredients. Bake until golden brown. Add stewed tomatoes, ketchup, and chicken broth. Continue baking for ½ hour. Place live lobster in a large pot. Remove sauce from oven and empty contents into lobster pot. Add water, cover, and simmer over medium heat 1 hour or until half of the liquid remains. Add the sherry, Maggi sauce, salt and pepper and simmer 3 minutes longer. Remove and shell the lobster and add meat to the sauce. Press through a strainer and reserve.

FLOGERA GREEK PASTRY

18 sheets of commercially prepared
    filo (strudle leaves)
Filling:
3 eggs, separated
1 pint milk
¼ cup flour
¼ cup cornstarch
1 teaspoon vanilla
½ cup sugar

Pinch of salt
1 cup butter, melted
Grated rind of ½ lemon
Syrup:
¾ cup sugar
½ cup water
1 teaspoon lemon juice
3 cloves (optional)
1 ounce brandy

To make the filling. Combine egg yolks and 1 cup of the milk in a mixing bowl. Beat with a whisk for a few seconds, then add the flour, cornstarch, and vanilla. Continue beating until smooth. In another bowl beat the egg whites with an electric mixer until frothy, then fold into the yolk mixture. Set aside. In a deep pot combine the remaining milk, sugar, salt, 1 teaspoon of butter, and grated lemon rind and bring to a boil, stirring continuously. Lower flame and slowly add the egg mixture. Continue to mix vigorously until mixture becomes very smooth. Remove from flame and cover, first with a paper towel and then with a lid. (This mixture must cool before pastry can be assembled.)

To make the syrup. In a small saucepan combine sugar, water, and lemon juice. Bring to a boil over high heat, stirring until sugar dissolves. Cook briskly for 15 minutes. Add the brandy and cloves and remove immediately from heat.

Brush butter on one full piece and one half piece of filo. Place smaller piece on top of the larger piece and place 3 full tablespoons of the filling mixture on the pastry. Fold the pastry in half and pinch the ends closed. Each piece should measure between 4½ and 5 inches in length. After all the filo is rolled, brush a little butter over the pastries and place them in a shallow pan to bake at 350° until golden brown. Remove from oven and cover with syrup. Serves 12.

(Czechoslovakian)
339 East 75th Street

HAM SALAD

½ pound sliced ham
½ pound sliced salami
4 medium dill pickles (peeled)
3 small green apples (peeled)
5 tablespoons mayonnaise

2 teaspoons prepared mustard
10 drops Worcestershire sauce
Juice of ½ lemon
Lettuce leaves, parsley, lemon wedges,
    and tomato slices for garnishing

Cut ham, salami, pickles, and apples into julienne strips. Mix together mayonnaise, mustard, Worcestershire sauce, and lemon juice. Combine all ingredients and mix well. Taste and add more mustard and/or lemon juice, if necessary. Chill overnight in the refrigerator. Serve on a bed of lettuce garnished with parsley, lemon wedges, and sliced tomatoes. Serves 4–5.

CAULIFLOWER SOUP

1 small head cauliflower
1½ quarts boiling water
2 tablespoons butter
4 tablespoons flour

2 tablespoons light cream
1 egg yolk
½ teaspoon mace
Salt to taste

Wash cauliflower and boil in salted water until almost tender. Remove from water and set aside, reserving water. Heat butter in soup pot until foamy, add flour, and cook over low heat for several minutes (do not brown). Using a wire whisk, stir in hot water used to cook the cauliflower and cook over medium heat until creamy—at least half an hour. Stir often so soup does not stick to bottom of pot. Separate cauliflower into bite-sized pieces and add to soup. Cook another 10 minutes over low heat. Mix together cream and egg yolk. Take soup off heat and add mace and salt to taste. Stir egg and cream mixture into soup just before serving. Serves 4-5.

ROAST DUCK VASATA STYLE

1 6-pound duckling	Pork bones, duck wings, and giblets
2 teaspoons coarse salt	Hot water
1 teaspoon caraway seeds	Cornstarch mixed with cold water

Preheat oven to 400°. Wash the duckling and rub both outside and inside with salt and caraway seeds. Place the bird in an open roasting pan on a bed of bones, add hot water to pan to a depth of 1 inch (more water may be added during cooking time so bones do not burn), and roast in hot oven for about 2½ hours or until tender. While roasting, turn duck every ½ hour and prick the skin all over with a sharp fork so the fat can run out. Baste with drippings. When roasted, the duckling should be golden brown and there should not be any fat under the skin. Remove duckling from pan and keep warm. Drain most of the fat from the pan, add hot water to the bones, and scrape sides of the pan. Cook in oven for 15 minutes longer. Strain gravy into a saucepan, bring to a boil on top of stove, and add about a teaspoon of cornstarch mixed with a tablespoon or so of cold water for each cup of liquid. Stir with a wire wisk and simmer for 15 minutes. Add salt to taste if necessary. If the gravy is too salty, add more water. Serves 4—5.

PALAČINKY
(Thin Pancakes)

1 cup milk	¼ teaspoon sugar
3 eggs	Clarified butter
10 tablespoons sifted flour	Small jar apricot jam heated with a
Grated rind from ¼ lemon	tablespoon of dark Jamaica rum
Pinch of salt	Vanilla-flavored powdered sugar

Mix milk and eggs together. Put flour in a mixing bowl, add lemon rind, salt, and sugar. Stir together and pour in milk and egg mixture. Beat on a low setting for about 5 minutes. Dough must be very thin and well mixed. Do not overbeat. (A wire whisk may be used instead of an electric mixer.) Heat a small, heavy skillet (about 6 inches across) until very hot, butter skillet with a basting brush and pour a little of the dough in center. Move skillet from side to side so that mixture covers the whole frying surface. When brown on one side, turn and brown the other. Stack palačinky on a warm plate as you fry them. When all are done, spread each with a little of the warm jam mixture and roll up. Sprinkle with powdered sugar and serve. Serves 4—5.

La Boîte Russe

(Russian)
St. Regis-Sheraton Hotel
Fifth Avenue
and 55th Street

PIROZHKI
(Meat-filled Pastry)

Pastry:
4 cups flour
½ teaspoon salt
½ pound butter, cut into ¼-inch bits
8 tablespoons chilled lard, cut into
   ¼-inch bits
8 to 12 tablespoons ice water

Filling:
4 tablespoons butter
3 cups onions, finely chopped
1½ pounds lean ground beef
3 hard-boiled eggs, finely chopped
6 tablespoons fresh dill, finely cut
2 teaspoons salt
¼ teaspoon black pepper

To make pastry. Combine the flour, salt, butter, and lard in a deep bowl. Use your fingers to blend flour and shortening together until the mixture looks like flakes of coarse meal. Sprinkle 8 tablespoons of ice water over the mixture, mix lightly with a fork, then roll dough into a large ball. If it crumbles, add up to 4 additional tablespoons of ice water, 1 tablespoon at a time, until the particles adhere to one another. Wrap the ball in wax paper and chill for an hour. On a lightly floured surface, shape the pastry into a rectangle 1-inch thick and roll it into a strip 21 inches long and 6 inches wide. Turn the pastry around and roll it out lengthwise into a second 21-inch by 6-inch strip. Fold into thirds and roll out the packet as before. Repeat this process twice more, ending with the folded packet. Wrap the dough in wax paper and refrigerate for at least one hour.

To make filling. Melt butter in a heavy, 10-inch skillet over a high heat. Lower heat, add onions, and cook for 8 to 10 minutes, stirring occasionally, until they are soft and transparent but not brown. Stir in the beef and, mashing the meat with a fork to break up any lumps, cook briskly until no traces of pink remain. Grind the meat and onion mixture through the finest blade of a meat grinder. (If a meat grinder is unavailable, chop finely.) In a large bowl combine meat with eggs, dill, salt, and pepper. Mix thoroughly and season further to taste.

Preheat oven to 400°. On a lightly floured surface, roll the dough into a circle about ⅛-inch thick. With a 3- to 3½-inch cookie cutter, cut out as many circles as you can. Gather the scraps into a ball and roll out again, cutting additional circles. Drop two tablespoons of filling in the center of each circle and flatten the filling slightly. Fold one side of the dough over the filling, almost covering it. Fold the two ends of the dough toward the center (about ½ inch) and, lastly, fold over the remaining side of the dough. Place the pirozhki side by side, with the seam side down, on a buttered baking dish. Bake for 30 minutes, or until golden brown. Serve with chicken or beef consommé—or separately as an appetizer. Yield: 40 pastries.

CHARLOTTE RUSSE

12 to 16 ladyfingers, split in half
   lengthwise
4 large egg yolks
½ cup sugar
1 cup milk
2-inch piece of vanilla bean
2 level teaspoons unflavored gelatin,
   softened in ¼ cup cold water

½ cup chilled sour cream
½ cup chilled heavy cream
Raspberry Puree:
2 10-ounce packages of frozen raspberries, defrosted and drained
2 tablespoons superfine sugar
1 tablespoon kirsch or other cher-
   ry-flavored brandy

Trim 12 of the ladyfinger halves, tapering them slightly at one end. Arrange these halves, side by side, curved sides down, on the bottom of a 1-quart charlotte mold with the tapered ends meeting in the center. Stand the remaining ladyfingers, curved side out, side by side, around the inside of the mold; if possible, avoid leaving any open spaces between them. Beat the egg yolks briefly in a mixing bowl with a whisk or an electric mixer. Still beating, gradually add the sugar and continue to beat until the mixture is thick and pale yellow and runs sluggishly off the beater when lifted from the bowl. In a small saucepan, warm the milk and vanilla bean over moderate heat until bubbles appear around the edges of the pan. Remove the bean and slowly pour the hot milk into the eggs, beating constantly. Cook over low heat, stirring constantly until the mixture thickens into a custard heavy enough to coat a spoon. Do not let the mixture boil or it will curdle. Remove from the stove and stir in softened gelatin. When the gelatin has completely dissolved, strain the custard through a fine sieve set over a large bowl. With a whisk or an electric mixer, whip together the sour cream and heavy cream until the mixture forms stiff peaks. Fill half of a large pot with ice cubes and cover with 2 inches of water. Set the bowl of custard into the pot and stir the custard with a metal spoon for at least five minutes, or until it is quite cold and beginning to thicken to a syrupy consistency. With a rubber spatula, gently fold the whipped cream in to the custard. Pour the mixture into the prepared mold, smooth the top with a spatula, cover with plastic wrap, and refrigerate for 4 to 5 hours.

To make raspberry puree. Using the back of a large wooden spoon, rub the raspberries through a fine sieve set over a mixing bowl. Stir the sugar and kirsch into the puree, cover tightly with plastic wrap, and refrigerate the mixture until ready to serve.

To unmold charlotte russe, invert a flat serving plate on top of the mold and, grasping the plate and mold firmly together, turn them over. Gently remove the mold and serve the charlotte russe with a bowl of raspberry puree on the side. Serves 6.

JINGHA TARHI
(Prawn Curry)

(Indian)
50 East 58th Street

2¼ pounds large shrimp	2 teaspoons ground coriander
½ cup peanut or vegetable oil	1 teaspoon ground cumin
1 large onion, chopped (about 1½ cups)	2 teaspoons paprika
	½ cup yogurt
½ teaspoon celery seed	2 tablespoons fresh coriander leaves, chopped
1 tablespoon finely minced garlic	
½ cup water	Juice of ½ lemon
1 teaspoon turmeric	Salt to taste

Shell and devein shrimps. Rinse and drain well and set aside. Heat oil in a deep saucepan and add onion. Cook about 10 minutes, stirring often. When onions turn golden brown, add celery seed, garlic, and half the water. Cook about 3 minutes and add salt, turmeric, ground coriander, cumin, and paprika. Cook, stirring, about 3 minutes more and add the yogurt and remaining water. Cook about 4 minutes, add the shrimp, and cook 8–10 minutes, stirring frequently. Cover and cook for another 10 minutes. Sprinkle with fresh coriander and lemon juice. Serve hot. Serves 6 or more.

BAKHARA PASANDI
(Lamb Curry)

2 pounds lean lamb, cut into 2-inch cubes
½ cup peanut or vegetable oil
1 large onion, coarsely grated
2 whole, unhusked cardamom seeds, or ½ teaspoon ground cardamom
½ teaspoon ground ginger

1 2-inch piece stick cinnamon
2 whole cloves
1 teaspoon minced garlic
2½ cups water
½ cup yogurt
½ cup heavy cream
Salt to taste

Heat the oil in a large, heavy saucepan and add onion. Cook, stirring, about 5 minutes and add cardamom, ginger, cinnamon, and cloves. Cook about 10 minutes longer, stirring frequently. When onion starts to brown, add the garlic and ⅔ cup water. Simmer briefly and add the yogurt and lamb, stirring to coat the pieces. Sprinkle with salt and cook over a high heat, stirring often, for 5 minutes. Cover and cook about 30 minutes (or until sauce is quite dry), stirring often. Add the remaining water and cover again. Cook 30 minutes longer, stirring often. Add cream. Cook uncovered about 15 minutes longer. Serves 4 to 6.

TANDOORI CHICKEN

1 3-pound frying or broiling chicken
Juice of 1 lime
¼ teaspoon red chili powder
1-inch piece of ginger, smashed
⅛ teaspoon garlic flakes

1 cup yogurt
1 tablespoon salad oil
½ teaspoon orange food coloring
Salt to taste
¼ teaspoon garlic powder, or ½

Remove skin and wash chicken well. Cut slits lengthwise across breast portion and breadthwise over legs. Sprinkle chicken with lime juice and salt and set aside. Blend spices and yogurt and mix well. Add oil and food coloring, then pass through a fine sieve. Smear mixture over surface of chicken and into slits. Soak the chicken in remaining batter, and refrigerate for 12 hours. Remove chicken from batter and drain. Wrap chicken in aluminum foil and roast in a moderate oven (350°) until fork-tender. Remove foil and brush chicken with a light coating of oil and then the remaining batter. Finish cooking uncovered. Serve hot, garnished with lime wedges. Serves 4.

RAMAYANA

(Indonesian)
123 West 52nd Street

GADO-GADO
(Cooked Salad)

Salad:
½ cup cooked cabbage, shredded
½ cup cooked carrots, sliced
½ cup cooked cut green beans
½ cup French-fried potatoes
1 tomato, sliced
1 cucumber, sliced
1 cup fried soya bean cake, sliced (optional)
2 cooked eggs, sliced (for garnish)

Sauce:
6 tablespoons peanut butter
¼ teaspoon garlic powder, or ½ teaspoon chopped garlic
1 bay leaf
1 teaspoon ground red pepper
1 cup water
1 teaspoon sugar
½ cup milk
1 slice of lemon
Salt to taste

After cooking all vegetables, set aside and prepare sauce. Sauté the garlic, bay leaf, and red pepper in peanut butter. Add water, sugar, and milk gradually. Add lemon slice. Cook over low heat, stirring continuously until thickened. Place in a serving bowl. Arrange the vegetables and soya bean slices in a platter. Garnish with the French-fried potatoes and sliced boiled egg. Serves 4.

SATE AJAM
(Chicken Shish Kebab)

Kebabs:
3 cups chicken, cut into 1½-inch cubes
20–25 skewers
¼ teaspoon garlic powder, or ½ teaspoon chopped garlic
½ teaspoon vinegar
½ cup water

Sauce:
4 tablespoons peanut butter
½ teaspoon chopped garlic
½ cup milk
½ cup chicken bouillon
1 teaspoon ground red pepper
1 teaspoon soy sauce
1 teaspoon sugar
1 bay leaf
Salt to taste

Put five cubes of chicken on each skewer. Combine the remaining ingredients. Dip the chicken in this mixture. Bake chicken in a preheated 450° oven for 15 minutes. Serve hot with special sauce. Serves 5–6.

To make sauce. Combine all ingredients. Cook over a low flame, stirring continuously. When sauce is thickened remove from heat and reserve.

BAKMI GORENG
(Fried Noodles)

½ pound thin egg noodles, cooked
¼ teaspoon garlic powder, or 1 tablespoon chopped garlic
Dash of ginger powder
½ teaspoon salt
¼ teaspoon pepper
1 cup meat or chicken, chopped
1 cup shrimp, chopped

½ cup butter
4 cabbage leaves, shredded
2 carrots, sliced
½ cup celery, chopped
½ cup tomatoes, chopped
2 bouillon cubes, diluted in 2 cups of warm water
2 tablespoons fried onion flakes

Combine spices with the chopped meat and shrimp. Sauté in the butter in a covered pan. Stir occasionally until done. Add the fresh vegetables and mix. Add the noodles and the bouillon. Mix, reduce heat, and simmer 5 minutes. Remove from fire. Serve hot, garnished with fried onion flakes. For a one-dish meal, noodles can be served with pickles and chili sauce. Serves 6 to 8.

SERIKAJA
(Steamed Banana Pudding)

3 eggs
1 cup sugar
1 cup milk

1 teaspoon vanilla
3 bananas, sliced

Beat the eggs. Add sugar, milk, and vanilla. Mix thoroughly. Add the sliced bananas. Put the mixture in a deep, covered dish. Steam for about 30 minutes until thickened. Serves 4.

EGGPLANT WITH GARLIC SAUCE

Uncle Tai's

HUNAN YUAN

(Chinese)
1059 Third Avenue

1 12-ounce eggplant
6 ounces pork, a boneless piece cut from the ham or loin
½ green pepper
½ red pepper
1/3 cup green scallion tops, finely chopped
4 cups vegetable oil
1 tablespoon peeled and minced ginger root
1 teaspoon minced garlic
¼ teaspoon crushed Szechuan peppercorns*
1 tablespoon prepared hot bean paste* or 1 tablespoon chili paste with garlic
½ teaspoon sesame seed oil

Marinade:
½ egg white
1 tablespoon dry sherry
Salt to taste
1 tablespoon cornstarch
Sauce:
2¾ teaspoons cornstarch dissolved in 2¾ teaspoons water
2½ tablespoons soy sauce
1 tablespoon dry sherry
1½ tablespoons vinegar
1½ tablespoons sugar
6 tablespoons chicken stock
¼ teaspoon MSG (optional)

Do in advance. Trim and freeze pork whole, removing it from the freezer 30 minutes before you are ready to cut it. When it is semifrozen, cut it with the grain into strips 1/6 inch wide and 2½ inches long. Place pork shreds in a medium-sized mixing bowl and add the egg white, dry sherry, and salt. Mix thoroughly but gently with your hand until the egg white is broken up and foams lightly. Now add the cornstarch and mix again until it is completely dissolved and no lumps remain. Cover and refrigerate until ready to cook. (The pork may be used after just 20 minutes of marinating, although the longer it marinates the smoother the texture becomes.) Peel the eggplant and cut in into large, lengthwise slices 2/3 of an inch thick. Cut the slices to finger-length size. Cut the peppers into 2-inch-long shreds, approximately 1/6 inch in width. Prepare sauce by mixing dissolved cornstarch with soy sauce, sherry, vinegar, sugar, stock, and MSG.

To cook. Heat vegetable oil in a wok to 350°. Add the eggplant and fry it for about 2 minutes until it colors lightly. Drain into a sieve, using the back of a large spoon or another sieve to press out all the oil the eggplant has absorbed. Return 3 cups of the oil to the wok and heat to 280°. Add the pork shreds and stir constantly with a pair of chopsticks so that the strands separate from each other. Continue cooking, stirring constantly, for 1 minute more, then drain into a sieve set over a pot to catch the oil. Return wok to the highest heat and

Note: Asterisks (*) above and in the following Oriental recipes indicate ingredients not generally available in American supermarkets. All are available in well-stocked Oriental food stores, however, or may be ordered by mail from the following specialty shops: Japanese Foodland, 2620 Broadway, New York, New York 10025; Katagiri and Co., Inc., 224 East 59th Street; New York, New York 10022; Miyako Oriental Food Store, 490 Main Street, Fort Lee, New Jersey 07024; Sam Bok Grocery, 2717 Broadway, New York, New York 10025.

add the ginger, garlic, Szechuan peppercorn, hot bean paste, and red and green peppers. Stir-fry for about 10 seconds. If wok is too dry, add a maximum of 1 tablespoon of vegetable oil (some oil will seep from the eggplant when added). Add the eggplant, pork shreds, and the premixed sauce (stir sauce from the bottom to redistribute cornstarch). Stir-fry gently so as not to break up the eggplant for about a minute until the sauce has thickened and the food is bubbling hot. Stir in the scallions. Turn off heat and mix in the sesame seed oil. Serves 4.

Saito

(Japanese)
305 East 46th Street

SHABU-SHABU

1–1½ pounds boneless shell steak or sirloin steak, cut into paper-thin slices (semifreezing steak before use will facilitate slicing)
1 medium-sized carrot, scraped and sliced thin
1 bunch watercress
4 small mushrooms, sliced into ⅛-inch pieces
1 small portion tofu (soy bean curd), cut into 1-inch cubes*
1 4-inch square dashi kombu (dried kelp; wash under running water before using)*
1 pound Chinese cabbage, cut into 1½-inch pieces*
2 large onions, cut into ¼-inch pieces
8 scallions, cut into 1½-inch pieces

2 small bamboo shoots, sliced in half and then into pieces ⅛-inch in length
4 ounces kishimen (wide Japanese noodles), cooked and drained (an 8-ounce can of shirataki, or yam noodles, may be substituted*)
Lemon Soy Sauce:
2 cups soy sauce
1 cup orange juice
1 cup lemon juice
Pinch of MSG (optional)
Sesame Soy Sauce:
½ cup sesame seeds
2 teaspoons sugar
3 tablespoons saké or mirin wine*
2 tablespoons soy sauce
Pepper

Shabu-shabu is beef and vegetables cooked in broth and served with a dipping sauce. Accompanied with steamed rice, it is a meal in itself. In all *nabe*—one-pot, do-it-yourself cooking—the cooking is done at the dinner table, although the uncooked food is sliced and arranged in advance. An electric skillet or a fondue pot are ideal for this style of cooking.

To cook kishimen. Bring 2 quarts of water to a boil and gently drop in the noodles. Bring to a boil again, lower heat, and cook for about 10 minutes, stirring occasionally. Drain in a colander and run cold water over noodles for a few minutes. Drain, cut noodles into thirds, and keep warm. (If shirataki is used, boil in about 1 cup of water for a few minutes, drain and reserve.)

To make lemon soy sauce. Combine all ingredients. Garnish with chopped scallions or shaved white radish.

To make sesame soy sauce. Warm sesame seeds and grind into a fine paste. Add other ingredients and mix well. Sprinkle with freshly ground pepper to taste.

When ready to serve, arrange meat, vegetables, bean curd, and noodles attractively on a large serving platter. Serve the dipping sauces in individual bowls. At the table, bring 4 cups of water to a boil in the skillet or fondue pot and drop in the dashi kombu. Adjust the heat so that the stock simmers (you may have to adjust the heat again several times during the meal). Each guest selects a piece of food from the communal platter and, using chopsticks or a fondue fork, swishes it about in the simmering broth until it is cooked to taste. (Cooking meat first will enhance the flavor of the broth.) Occasionally spoon off the surface scum. If the broth boils down, add a cup of boiling water. Serves 4.

CHAWAN MUSHI

2 medium-sized raw shrimps, peeled deveined, and cut in half lengthwise
½ medium-sized chicken breast, boned and cut into thin slices
24 ginkgo nuts
24 nameko (tiny Japanese mushrooms)* or 2 small mushrooms sliced
4 sprigs mitsuba (fragrant Japanese herb)* or watercress
4 slices of kamaboko (fish cake)*

3 medium-sized eggs
2 tablespoons usukuchi shoyu (light soy sauce)*
1 tablespoon mirin wine*
Pinch of MSG (optional)
Dashi-jiri (Basic Soup Stock):
3½ cups cold water
1 3-inch square dashi kombu (dried kelp)*
3 ounces preflaked katsuobushi (dried shaved bonito)*

Chawan Mushi is a steamed egg custard containing bits of seafood, chicken, and vegetables. It is often served as a soup course in a small covered soup bowl.

To make dashi-jiri. Place dashi kombu in cold water and bring to a boil over a high flame. Remove kombu and stir in the katsuobushi and turn off heat. Let stock rest undisturbed for a few minutes until the katsuobushi sinks to the bottom of the pan. Skim off any surface scum with a large spoon. Strain through a double thickness of cheesecloth over a sieve.

Prepare shrimp and chicken by quickly cooking in boiling salted water. Distribute shrimp, chicken, nuts, and vegetables and kamaboko evenly in individual custard bowls. Beat eggs well, but not to a froth. Stir in 3 cups dashi-jiri, the usukuchi shoyu, mirin, and a dash of MSG. Gently pour equal amounts of liquid into the custard bowls (do not fill to the top), and carefully spoon off any surface bubbles. Before covering with lid, place a piece of folded cheesecloth over the cup to absorb moisture (which causes bubbling and an uneven texture in the custard). Place custard cups in a steamer and bring water to a boil. Steam, covered, over a moderate heat for about 10 minutes. Remove cheesecloth and serve. Serves 4.

Shinbashi

(Japanese)
280 Park Avenue

EBISHINJO
(Shrimp Balls)

1 pound medium-sized raw shrimp (16 to 20 per pound), shelled and deveined
½ cup onion, very finely chopped
1½ tablespoons cornstarch

2 egg yolks
Sufficient cornstarch to coat shrimp balls
Vegetable oil

Flatten the shrimp with the side of a knife, chop thoroughly, and put into a mixing bowl. Set the finely chopped onions in the middle of a square of cheesecloth, fold closed, and squeeze out onion juice. Discard juice and place onions in a second bowl. Add the measured cornstarch to the chopped onions and mix well. Add shrimp and mix again. Finally, add the egg yolks to the shrimp-onion combination. Shape the mixture into 16 small balls. Coat the shrimp balls lightly with unmeasured cornstarch, shaking off excess. Indent the shrimp balls with your thumb so that they are somewhat flattened (like a doughnut without a hole). Heat the vegetable oil in a deep-fat fryer to 375°. Fry the shrimp balls for about two minutes, turning once. Drain on a paper towel. Serve piping hot with wedges of lemon or Worcestershire sauce. (May be served as an appetizer or as a side dish.) Serves 4.

NASU NO SHIGIYAKI
(Broiled Eggplant)

2 medium-sized eggplants, unpeeled
1 cup akadashi miso (red soybean
   paste)
7–8 tablespoons sugar, depending
   upon saltiness of the miso used

4 tablespoons saké or pale dry sherry
2 egg yolks, thoroughly beaten
3½ tablespoons vegetable oil

Prepare the miso paste by mixing the red miso with sugar, saké, and egg yolks in a small saucepan. Stir while cooking over a moderate flame until sugar has dissolved. When the mixture forms a thick paste, remove from heat and set aside. Wash the eggplants and trim both ends. Cut the eggplants in half lengthwise, then remove a small slice from the round side of each half so that it will lie flat. Using a very sharp paring knife, completely separate meat from skin of eggplant, being careful not to pierce the skin. Cut crosses on the top surface. Preheat oven to broil. Brush the vegetable oil on all sides of the eggplants and broil for 4–5 minutes on each side. (Timing depends upon size of the eggplant). Take the eggplants out of the broiler and with a spatula spread the miso paste rather thickly on top of them. Replace under the broiler and broil for about half a minute to heat the paste (watch carefully because miso paste burns very quickly under the broiler). To serve, place eggplant on individual dishes and sprinkle with toasted sesame seeds.

Note: Any miso paste that is left over may be kept in a covered jar and refrigerated for more than a month. If the sauce has been refrigerated for a long period of time, however, add a tablespoon of saké, mix, and reheat slowly before using. Serves 4.

BEEF TERIYAKI

4 ½-pound club steaks or rib
   steaks with bone removed

Teriyaki Sauce:
1½ cups saké or pale dry sherry
½ cup sugar
1½ cups soy sauce

Prepare the teriyaki sauce first by mixing the saké and sugar in a saucepan over moderate flame until the sugar has dissolved. Turn off the heat and ignite the saké mixture with a match, shaking pan until the flame dies. Add the soy sauce and bring mixture to a boil. Continue boiling until syrupy and reduced to about 2 cups. Pour sauce into a bowl large enough to dip steaks. Preheat the broiler (if you are using a hibachi or grill, be sure the coals are very hot). Dip the steak into teriyaki sauce, coating the meat thoroughly. Broil or barbecue to desired doneness, dipping the meat into the sauce again when it is turned. To serve, slice steak into ¾-inch slices and place on a warmed plate. Pour a little of the warmed teriyaki sauce over the steaks and garnish with parsley. Serve with hot rice. Serves 4.

The
COACH
HOUSE

(American)
110 Waverly Place

FRESH CRAB MEAT WITH PROSCIUTTO

48 thin slices prosciutto
1½ pounds lump crab meat
1½ cups butter
2 teaspoons Worcestershire sauce

1 cup white wine
Juice of 2 lemons
4 tablespoons finely chopped parsley
Black pepper

Arrange 4 slices of prosciutto on a flat surface, each slice slightly overlapping the next one. In the center place one tablespoon crab meat. From the narrow end, roll up prosciutto like a cigar. Repeat with remaining prosciutto and crab meat to make 12 rolls. In a large skillet, melt the butter; place the prosciutto rolls in the butter and cook over medium heat. (When heated, the ham will cling to the crab meat.) Turn over only once, and cook for a few minutes more. Transfer rolls to a warm platter. To the juices remaining in the skillet, add Worcestershire sauce, wine, lemon juice, and parsley; reduce over a rapid fire. Pour over prosciutto rolls and serve hot with freshly ground pepper. Serves 6.

ARTICHOKE HEARTS À LA GRECQUE

8 large artichokes
2 lemons, cut in half
2 large onions, sliced in rings
4 carrots
2 tablespoons fresh chopped dill
Salt
10 peppercorns

½ bottle dry white wine
1 cup olive oil
Juice of 4 lemons
2½ tablespoons flour
2 tablespoons chopped parsley for garnishing

Cut off artichoke stems, remove outer leaves exposing the hearts. Cut off about 1½ inches of the top, and rub each artichoke heart immediately with lemon to prevent discoloration. Scrape off fuzz from the artichoke hearts and let them soak for a while in salted water to which the juice of 2 lemons and 2 tablespoons of flour have been added. (This helps to keep the artichokes green.) Rinse and drain well. Place hearts—bottoms up—in a saucepan, add the onions, carrots, dill, salt, peppercorns, wine, and water to cover. Beat the olive oil with the juice of 2 lemons and 1 teaspoon of flour. Add to artichokes. Place a piece of buttered paper over the top, put the lid on, and cook slowly until the artichokes are very tender, about one hour. To serve, place chilled artichokes—bottoms down—on a plate and surround them with other vegetables of your choice. Sprinkle with fresh parsley. Serves 4.

BLACK BEAN SOUP

4 cups washed and sorted black beans, soaked in cold water over-night
5 quarts cold water
½ cup butter
3 celery stalks, finely chopped
3 large onions, finely chopped
2½ tablespoons flour
½ cup parsley, finely chopped

Rind and bone of a cooked smoked ham
3 leeks, thinly sliced
2 bay leaves
1 tablespoon salt
½ teaspoon freshly ground black pepper
1 cup dry Madeira wine
2 hard-boiled eggs, finely chopped
2–3 lemons, thinly sliced

Drain beans. Place in a large kettle with cold water. Cook over low heat for one-and-a-half hours. Melt butter in saucepan. Sauté celery and onions for 8 minutes or until tender. Stir in flour and parsley, cooking and stirring for about 1 minute. Gradually stir this mixture into the beans. Add the ham bone and rind, leeks, bay leaves, and salt and pepper. Simmer for 4 hours. Press beans through a strainer or food mill. Return beans to kettle with broth. Add Madeira wine and heat soup. Remove from stove. Stir in hard-cooked eggs. Float a slice of lemon on each portion. Serve hot. Serves 16.

COACH HOUSE CHOCOLATE CAKE

Cake layers:
4 cups flour
1½ cups butter
½ pound Maillard Eagle sweet
   chocolate*
1/3 cup warm water
½ teaspoon salt

Filling:
2 cups heavy cream
1 pound Maillard Eagle sweet
   chocolate*
Chocolate curls
Confectioners' sugar

To make the cake layers. Place the flour in a bowl. Using a pastry blender, two knives or the fingertips, work the butter into the flour as though making pastry until the mixture resembles coarse oatmeal. Do not allow the butter to become oily. Melt the chocolate very slowly in a double boiler. Beat in water and salt until mixture is smooth. Fold the chocolate mixture into the flour and butter. Divide the dough into three parts, wrap each part in wax paper, and chill 20 minutes in the refrigerator. Roll each third of the dough, in turn, between sheets of wax paper, making a rectangle about 8 by 12 inches. Peel off the top layer of paper, fold the dough in thirds like a business letter, peeling away the bottom layer of paper as you go. Wrap in fresh wax paper and chill 20 minutes. Repeat twice more with each section of dough and chill until very firm, about 2 hours. Preheat oven to 325°. Roll each section of dough between wax paper and remove the top sheet. Using a sharp knife, cut a 9- to- 10-inch circle of dough from each rolled section, leaving a round of wax paper beneath the layer. Place the circle, paper side down, on an ungreased baking sheet. Bake 30 minutes or until done. Cool for 5 minutes, remove wax paper, and finish cooling on the sheet. Repeat with the other sections of dough.

To make the filling. When the cake layers are completely cold, place the cream in a chilled bowl set in a slightly larger bowl filled with ice. Melt the chocolate very slowly in a double boiler. Whip the cream until stiff. When the chocolate is melted but still only lukewarm, fold it into the whipped cream. Spread the chocolate cream filling between the layers (it will be quite thick). Sprinkle the top with confectioners' sugar and garnish with chocolate curls. Chill well. The cake should be removed from the refrigerator at least an hour before it is to be served. Use a sharp serrated knife for cutting. (The cake freezes well.) Serves 12 to 16.

*Maillard Eagle sweet chocolate is available at most specialty food stores and supermarkets; another fine, sweet chocolate may be substituted.

Mr.&Mrs.
Foster's Place

(American)
242 East 81st Street

BROILED CHICKEN LIVERS WITH WINE SAUCE AND HERB TOAST

½ pound chicken livers
4 shallots
1 ounce dry sherry
1 ounce Madeira
½ teaspoon salt

⅛ teaspoon freshly ground pepper
2 drops Tabasco sauce
Paprika
6 slices of bread
Parsley for garnish

Livers and sauce. Wash, drain, and trim chicken livers. Cut each liver into three pieces. Mince shallots and sprinkle them over the livers in a bowl, tossing to flavor. Beat dry sherry, Madeira, salt, pepper, and Tabasco into melted butter. Pour wine-butter sauce over the livers, tossing well with a fork to coat all sides. Place livers on a broiler pan, leaving a little space between pieces. Dust lightly with paprika. Broil close to high heat until golden. Turn livers with a spatula, dust again lightly with paprika and broil until golden brown. Serve in 6 small hot crocks, spooning the remaining wine-butter sauce over the livers. Garnish with chopped parsley. Serves 6.

Herb toast. Toast 6 slices of bread, crusts removed. Cut into points. Dip points into melted herb butter, using herbs of your choice. Place in hot oven to crisp and serve very hot.

CHICKEN CURRY SOUP

6 cups chicken stock
1 cup celery, finely chopped
1 cup cooked chicken, cut into julienne strips
1½ teaspoons curry powder blended in 3 tablespoons cold water

1 large, tart apple, grated
1 cup baby green peas, cooked for 2 minutes and drained
1½ tablespoons lemon juice
Crushed roasted peanuts

Heat chicken stock. Add celery, cook 2 minutes, then add chicken, curry, and apple. Bring to a boil and simmer 5 minutes. When ready to serve add cooked peas and lemon juice. Heat, correct seasonings, and served garnished with crushed roasted peanuts. Serves 6.

FILLET OF BEEF WITH BURGUNDY SAUCE

2½ pounds trimmed beef fillet, all fat removed
2 medium-sized onions, sliced
3 medium-sized carrots, scraped and sliced into rounds
6 stalks of celery, string and cut into ¼-inch pieces
2 cups cooked white kidney beans, well drained
½ teaspoon sugar
½ cup water
6–8 tablespoons butter
24 small toast points
Watercress or parsley for garnishing

Burgundy Wine Sauce:
2 cups Burgundy wine
6 cups concentrated, fat-free beef stock
1 clove garlic, crushed
¼ teaspoon powdered thyme
½ bay leaf
1 tablespoon tomato puree
1 tablespoon arrowroot
1½ tablespoons soft butter
2 tablespoons butter
¼ teaspoon sugar

Cut fillet into 24 equal slices and gently pound flat between sheets of wax paper. Place vegetables, except kidney beans, in a heavy pan. Sprinkle with sugar and add water. Bring to a boil. Cover with tight-fitting lid, reduce heat, and simmer for 6 to 8 minutes. (Vegetables should remain crisp.) While vegetables are cooking, melt 1/3 of the butter in a large skillet. When it bubbles, place 8 slices of meat in the skillet and sauté only long enough for one side of each to heat through. Turn and sauté other side until the meat is cooked rare. Keep warm.

Discard fat, melt another third of the butter, and sauté more meat slices. Repeat with fresh butter until all the pieces are cooked.

To make sauce. Simmer wine until reduced to 1 cup. In a separate saucepan combine beef stock, garlic, thyme, bay leaf, and tomato puree and simmer for ½ hour. Strain; discard solids. Combine stock and wine. Blend the arrowroot into 1½ tablespoons soft butter and add bit by bit to sauce, stirring constantly over low heat until sauce is thickened (sauce is quite thin and more arrowroot can be used if desired). Add sugar. Correct seasonings. Just before serving swirl in two tablespoons butter, a little at a time. Do not allow to boil.

To assemble. Place a mound of beans and vegetables in the center of 6 hot plates. Place 4 slices of meat around each mound. Pour half a cup of Burgundy sauce over all. Finally, place 4 toast points on each plate and garnish with watercress or parsley. Serves 6.

MRS. FOSTER'S FROSTY LIME PIE

Crust:
1½ cups graham cracker crumbs
¼ cup superfine sugar
¼ cup butter, room temperature
Filling:
5 eggs, separated
¾ cup superfine sugar
2 teaspoons grated lime rind

⅔ cup fresh-squeezed and strained lime juice
⅛ teaspoon salt
Topping:
1½ cups heavy cream, whipped
Thin slices of lime or fresh strawberries
Sugar

To prepare the crust. Place graham cracker crumbs and sugar in a bowl. Add the butter and mix with a wooden spoon to blend well. Press the mixture evenly into a 9-inch pie plate with the fingertips or use an 8-inch pie plate to press down the mixture. Bake for 10 minutes at 350°. Cool to room temperature.

To make the filling. Beat the yolks in the top portion of a double boiler until very thick. Gradually beat in ½ cup of sugar until mixture is very pale and thick and forms a rope when dropped from the beater. Stir in the lime juice and rind and heat over simmering water, stirring until mixture coats the back of the spoon. Do not allow to boil. Turn into a large bowl and cool to room temperature. When the yolk mixture is cool, beat the egg whites with salt until soft peaks form. Gradually beat in the remaining sugar until the mixture is stiff and glossy. Stir 1/3 of this meringue into the cooked yolk mixture. Fold in remaining meringue until evenly distributed. Turn into cooled graham cracker pie shell and bake 15 minutes or until lightly tinged with brown. Cool, chill, and freeze. Once frozen, cover with plastic wrap and keep frozen until just before serving. Remove from the freezer 10 minutes before serving, cover with whipped cream, and garnish with lime slices or fresh strawberries dipped in sugar.

Note: Pie will keep frozen two to three weeks. If a sweeter pie is desired, cut down the lime juice to ½ cup. Leftover pie can be frozen provided it has not been completely defrosted. Pie can also be served chilled and not frozen. Serves 8–10.

Selected Bibliography

American Heritage Editors and Helen McCully Associates. *The American Heritage Cookbook*. New York: American Heritage Publishing Co., 1969.

Balsdon, J.P.V.D. *Life and Leisure in Ancient Rome*. New York: McGraw-Hill, 1969.

Brillat-Savarin, Jean-Anthelme. *The Philosopher in the Kitchen (La Physiologie du Goût)*. Baltimore, Md.: Penguin Books, 1970.

Dallas, E.S. *Kettner's Book of the Table*. New York: Centaur House Inc., 1968.

Davis, William Stearns. *A Day in Old Athens*. Boston: Allyn & Bacon, 1914.

Earle, Alice Monroe. *Home Life in Colonial Days*. London: Macmillan Ltd., 1898.

Erlanger, Philippe. *The Age of Courts and Kings*. New York: Doubleday, 1970.

Escoffier, Auguste. *The Escoffier Cook Book*. New York: Crown Publishers, 1941.

Fisher, M.F.K. *The Art of Eating*. New York: World Publishing Co., 1954.

Guy, Christian. *An Illustrated History of French Cuisine*. New York: Bramhall House, 1962.

Hacker, Louis M. *The Shaping of the American Tradition*. New York: Columbia University Press, 1947.

Hale, William H. *The Horizon Cookbook*. New York: American Heritage Publishing Co., 1968.

Lewis, W.H. *The Splendid Century*. New York: Doubleday-Anchor, 1957.

Lo, Kenneth. *Chinese Food*. Baltimore, Md.: Penguin Books, 1972.

Marolius, Sidney. *The Great American Food Hoax*. New York: Walker & Co., 1971.

Martin, Joan and Peter. *Japanese Cooking*. New York: Signet Books, 1970.

McNeill, William H. *The Rise of the West*. Chicago: University of Chicago Press, 1963.

Montagné, Prosper. *Larousse Gastronomique*. New York: Crown Publishers, 1966.

Polo, Marco. *The Travels of Marco Polo*. New York: Liveright Publishing Co., 1926.

Quennell, C.H.B. and Marjorie. *Archaic Greece*. New York: G.P. Putnam's Sons, 1931.

Root, Waverly. *The Food of Italy*. New York: Atheneum Publishers, 1971.

Street, Julian. *Where Paris Dines*. New York: Doubleday, Doran & Co., 1929.

Tannahill, Reay. *Food in History*. New York: Stein & Day Publishers, 1973.

Wason, Betty. *Cooks, Gluttons, and Gourmets*. New York: Doubleday, 1962.

Picture Credits

The Editors would like to thank the following individuals and organizations for their invaluable assistance:

Russell Ash, London
Jane de Cabanyes, Madrid
Hunt Botanical Library, Pittsburgh—Kathryn Daniels, Bernadette Callery
Barbara Nagelsmith, Paris
New York Public Library, Rare Book Division—Maud Cole
Lynn Seiffer, New York

The following abbreviations are used:
MMA   —Metropolitan Museum of Art
RBD, NYPL—Rare Book Division, New York Public Library
(S)   —(Scala)

HALF TITLE Symbol designed by Jay J. Smith Studio. FRONTISPIECE Mosaic by Gaspar Homar. Museum of Modern Art, Barcelona (Oronoz)

CHAPTER 1 **6** Minoan pottery. Heraklion Museum (Josephine Powell) **8** Cave painting from Remigia Castellon, Spain (Newsweek) **9** Engraved bone from Lortet, Hautes-Pyrenees, France. Musée des Antiquites Nationales, St. Germain-en-Laye (Lauros-Giraudon) **10** Phyrgian pottery from Child's Tomb, Gordium. Ankara Museum (Josephine Powell) **11** Minoan pottery from Vasiliki. Heraklion Museum (Josephine Powell) **12** Tisza culture figure from Brudgos, Serbia.

National Museum, Belgrade. **13** Medallions, Greek culture. Both: Kabul Museum (Josephine Powell)

CHAPTER 2 **14** Detail of a painting from the Tomb of Two Sculptors, Thebes, 18th Dynasty. MMA **16** top, Stele of Nen-waf, 18th Dynasty. MMA, Rogers Fund, 1912; bottom, Relief from Tell el Armaneh, 18th Dynasty. MMA, Gift of Edward S. Harkness, 1921. **17** Wall painting from the Tomb of Nakht, 18th Dynasty. MMA **18–19** (Eliot Elisofon, Museum of African Art) **19** Assyrian relief of Ashur-nasir-apal II, from Kalhu, Nimrud, 9th century. MMA, Gift of John D. Rockefeller, Jr. 1932. **20–21** Elgin Marble. British Museum. **21** left, Red figure amphora from Athens, 5th century. B.C. MMA, Gift of Samuel G. Ward, 1875; right, Black figure amphora from Agrigento, 6th century B.C. MMA, Pulitzer Bequest, 1947. **22** Tarquinia Museum (S) **23** British Museum (Michael Holford) **24** left, Etruscan bronze cauldron, 7th century B.C. MMA, Pulitzer Bequest, 1954; right, Etruscan bronze colander, 6th century B.C., MMA, Fletcher Fund, 1934. **25** National Archaeological Museum, Naples (Parisio) **26** left, Ostia Museum; right, National Archaeological Museum, Reggio Calabria (S) **26–27** MMA, Fletcher Fund, 1925. **27** Both: Ostia Museum. **28** Museo Mandralisca, Cefalu (S) **28–29** National Museum, Naples. **30–31** Mausoleo di S. Costanza, Rome (S) **31** National Archaeological Museum Naples (Parisio)

CHAPTER 3 **32** *Wedding at Cana*, by the Parement Master, 14th century, BNP, N.A. Lat. 3093 fol 67v. **34** Labors of the months, 809. Osterreichische Nationalbibliothek, Vienna, Cod 387 fol 90v. **35** Monastery with vivarium, *ca.* 1000. Staatsbibliothek, Bamberg, Ms. Patr. 61, fol 29v. **36** Guillaume de Saint-Pathus, *Vie et Miracles de Saint Louis*, Paris, 1330–40. BNP, Ms Fr. 5716 fol 137. **37** (S) **38** Both: Bodleian Library, Oxford **39** Gaston Phebus, *Le Livre de la Chasse*, 1405. BNP, Ms. Fr. 616, fol 67. **40** All: *Teatrum Sanitatis*. Biblioteca Casanatense, Ms. 4182 (Vivarelli) **41** *Tacuinum Sanitatis*, Lombardy, 1350–1400. Osterreichische Nationalbibliothek, Vienna Ms. Ser. Nov 2.644 fol 71. **42 & 43** Labors of the months of June and May, by Maestro dei Mesi, 1406. Both: Castello del Buonconsiglio, Trento (S) **44** top, Cathedral Museum, Ferrara (S); bottom left, *Tacuinum Sanitatis*, Lombardy, 1350–1400. Osterreichische Nationalbibliothek, Vienna Ms. Ser. Nov. 2.644 fol 54v.; bottom right, *The Drunkenness of Noah*, by Giotto and Andrea Pisano, Duomo, Florence (Archivio B) **45** Labor of the month of August, by Maestro dei Mesi, 1406. Castello del Buonconsiglio, Trento (S) **46–47** Cristoforo Zavattari, *Banquet*. Duomo, Monza (S) **48** Castello di Gssogne (Studio Pizzi) **49** Detail from Filippo Lippi, *Madonna del Ceppo*. Galeria Communale, Prato (S) **50** Castello di Gssogne (Archivio B) **51** Fresco of the School of Ghirlandaio. S. Martino dei Buonomini, Florence (S) **52** left, Bartolomeo Scappi, *Cuoco Secreto di Papa Pio Quinto*, Venice, 1570; right, Bartolomeo Scappi, *Dell Arte del Cucinare . . .* , Venice, 1643. **52–53** Christoforo de Messi Sbugo, *Banchetti Compositione de Vivande . . .* , Ferrara, 1549. **53** Bartolomeo Scappi, *Cuoco Secreto di Papa Pio Quinto*, Venice, 1570.

CHAPTER 4 **54** Le Testu, *Cosmographie Universelle*, 16th century. Bibliothèque de la Guerre, Paris, fol. 32v. (Giraudon) **56** Jan Grevembroch, *Marco Polo*. Museo Correr, Venice, Ms. Grademigo Dolfin 191, vol 1. **57** Marco Polo, *Le Livre des Merveilles*, Boucicaut workshop, 14th century. BNP, Ms. Fr. 2810 fol 84. **58** top, Theodor de Bry, *America . . .* , 1590. RBD, NYPL; bottom, Andre Thevet, *La Cosmographie Universelle . . .* , Paris, 1575. British Museum. **59** Theodor de Bry, *America . . .* , 1590. RBD, NYPL **60–61** Indian cushion cover, 17th century. MMA, Rogers Fund, 1928. **62 & 63** All: Elizabeth Blackwell, *A Curious Herbal . . .* , London, 1739. Hunt Botanical Library. **64** Elizabeth Blackwell, *A Curious Herbal . . .* , London, 1739. Hunt Botanical Library. **64–65** English coffeehouse, 1668. British Museum. **66** left, BNP, Ms. Arabe 5847 fol 47v; top, Philippe Dufour, *Tractatus Novi . . .* , Paris, 1685. RBD, NYPL **67** *London Magazine*, 1774. Library of Congress.

CHAPTER 5 **68** Theodor de Bry, *America . . .* , 1590. RBD, NYPL **72** Zapotec funerary urn. Musée de l'Homme, Paris. **71** Colima figures, 100 –900. National

Museum of Anthropology, Mexico City. **72** Theodor de Bry, *America* . . . , 1590. RBD, NYPL **73** Elizabeth Blackwell, *A Curious Herbal* . . . , London, 1739. Hunt Botanical Library. **74** Jean Baptiste du Tertre, *Histoire Generale des Antilles*, Paris, 1667. Arents Collection, NYPL **75** top, Arents Collection, NYPL; bottom, Denis Diderot, *Encyclopedie, ou Dictionnaire Raisonne*, Paris, 1751–80. Arents Collection, NYPL **76 & 77** Theodor de Bry, *America* . . . , 1590. RBD, NYPL **78** top, John Gerard, *Herball* . . . , London, 1636. RBD, NYPL; bottom, Theodor de Bry, *America* . . . , 1590. RBD, NYPL **79** top, Theodor de Bry, *America* . . . , 1590. RBD, NYPL; bottom, Robert Johnson, *Nova Britannia* . . . , London, 1609. RBD, NYPL **80** Private Collection.

CHAPTER 6 **82** Jean François de Troy, *Le Déjeuner d'Huitres*. Musée Condé, Chantilly (Giraudon) **84** *Le Viandier de* . . . *Taillevent*, 1326–95. **86** BNP **87** *Tournament de Sandricourt*, 1493. Cabinet des Dessins, Louvre (Archives Photographiques) **88** BNP **89** Both: BNP **90–91** *Le Marche a la Volaille* . . . , 1650. Musée Carnavalet, Paris (Pizzi) **93** BNP **94** Ca' Rezzonico, Venice (S) **96** Charles Carter, *The Complete Practical Cook* . . . , London, 1730. Astor, Lenox & Tilden Foundations, NYPL **98–99** Jan Davidsz. de Heem, *Still Life*. MMA, Charles B. Curtis Fund, 1912. **99** Pieter Brueghel, *Peasant Wedding*. Kunsthistorisches Museum, Vienna (Meyer) **100** Abel Grimmer, *Autumn*. Musée Royal des Beaux-Arts, Antwerp (S) **101** top, Conrad Hagger, *Neues Saltzburgisches Koch-buch* . . . , Augsburg, 1719. Astor, Lenox & Tilden Foundations, NYPL; bottom, J. Van Boeckhorst and F. Snyders, *The Old Fish Merchant*, Casa di Rubens, Antwerp. **102** Hans Wertingen, *Month of August*. Germanisches Nationalmuseum, Nürnberg (S) **102–103** Jacob Phillip Hackert, *Der Sommer*. Germanisches Nationalmuseum, Nürnberg. **103** Peter Wagner, *Kuchenmeisterei* . . . , Nürnberg, 1536. Astor, Lenox & Tilden Foundations, NYPL **105** Boris Kustodiev, *Moscow Cafe*, 1916. Tretyakov Gallery, Moscow (S) **106** Jean-Baptiste-Simeon Chardin, *The Kitchen Maid*. National Gallery of Art, Washington, Samuel H. Kress Collection.

CHAPTER 7 **108** Tour d'Argent, Paris (Josse) **111** BNP **112–13** John Nash, *The Royal Pavilion at Brighton*, London, 1827. Cooper-Hewitt Museum of Decorative Arts. **114** Antoine Carême, *L'Art de la Cuisine Française*, Paris, 1854. **114–15** Antoine Carême, *Le Pâtissier Royal*, Paris, 1854. **116** BNP **117** top, BNP; bottom, Eugene Guerard, *Café Tortoni and the Cafe de Paris*. Musée Carnavalet, Paris (Josse) **118 & 119** All: BNP **120** Grimod de La Reynière, *Almanach des Gourmands*, Paris, 1810. **121** left, Grimod de La Reynière, *Manuel des Amphitryons*, Paris, 1808.; right, Jean-Anthelme Brillat-Savarin, *Physiologie du Goût* . . . , Paris, 1864. **122** Jean Beraud, *La Pâtisserie*. Musée Carnavalet, Paris (Josse) **123** left, BNP; right, Hotel Ritz, Paris **124** top (Culver Pictures); bottom, Tour d'Argent, Paris (Josse) **125** Both: (Roger-Viollet)

CHAPTER 8 **126** *Les Traits de la Vie des Empereurs Chinois*. BNP, OE5a, fol 46. **128** Tomb pottery, Han Dynasty. Victoria and Albert Museum, London. **129** Tomb pottery, Six Dynasties. MMA, Rogers Fund, 1925. **130** Ivory brush holder, 17th century. Collection of the King of Sweden. **130–31** Chiu Ying, *Palindrome of Sustai*. British Museum. **132** top, Liu Kuan-tao, *Whiling Away the Summer*. William Rockhill Nelson Gallery, Kansas City; bottom, The Taft Museum, Cincinnati. **133** top, Collection of the King of Sweden; bottom, MMA, Gift of John D. Rockefeller, Jr., 1945. **134** Victoria and Albert Museum, London. **135** Both: Percival David Collection, London. **136** J. B. Duhalde, *Description* . . . *de l'Empereur* . . . , Paris, 1735. **137** Al Hasani, *Jahangir*, 1608. Freer Gallery of Art, Washington. **138–39** *Ramayama*, Northern India, 1650. British Library, Oriental Ms. Add 15.296 fol 71. **140** National Museum, Tokyo. **141** *Rice Fields*, 17th century. National Museum, Tokyo. **142–43** top, *Life of the Samurai*, 14th century. Okura Shukokan Museum, Tokyo; bottom, Karatsu pottery. MMA, Gift of Howard Mansfield, 1936.

CHAPTER 9 **144** (B. Trutmann) **146** (Sun Luck East) **147** (Joel Brunerie) **149** (Pino dal Gal) **150** (MacDonald's Corporation) **152** Giuseppe Arcimboldo, *Summer*, 1563. Kunsthistorisches Museum, Vienna.

Index

Index to Recipes